Beginning
Windows® 8.1
And Microsoft
Office® 2013

Kiel Emerson

Author: Kiel Emerson

ISBN: 1499797672
ISBN-13: 978-1499797671

First Printing June 2014
For ordering and other information, contact:
Compare Computers L.L.C.
P.O. Box 1211
Hays, KS 67601
support@comparecomputers.net
www.comparecomputers.net

DEDICATION

This book is dedicated to my incredible family, for all of your love and encouragement.

KIEL EMERSON

Introduction

With Windows 8.1, Microsoft has worked to improve a number of features from previous versions of the operating system. The Start Menu from Windows 7 has been removed in favor of a Start Screen with live tiles. The Start Screen in Windows 8.1 fills the entire window and allows for an interactive, customizable screen of programs. The User Account Control, added after Windows XP, adds an additional defense against malicious software and unauthorized changes. Internet Explorer 11 provides support for HTML5 and CSS3.0, as well as numerous security enhancements.

Microsoft has also made significant changes to the user interface in Windows 8.1 compared to when Windows 8 was first released. The Start Button was added back to the Taskbar in Windows 8.1 after its removal in Windows 8. Windows 8.1 features faster boot up times and faster overall performance than Windows Vista and Windows 7. System requirements have decreased with Windows 8.1 from when Windows 8 was first released, allowing the new operating system to run well on less powerful hardware. Those familiar with previous versions of Windows will find many familiar elements in Windows 8.1, and after reading this guide, be aware of the new features and how to comfortably work with them on a daily basis.

A quick note on Windows RT- this operating system is a version of Windows 8.1 that runs on ARM CPU's. Windows RT looks similar to Windows 8.1, but is only able to run apps from the Windows Store. While there is a traditional desktop environment in Windows RT, just as there is in Windows 8.1, you are currently not able to install programs other than those available from the Windows Store.

In this book we will explore the layout and features of Windows 8.1, explain how to perform common tasks in the OS, and get an overview of Office 2013 and other programs commonly run on Windows 8.1.

KIEL EMERSON

Chapter 1 - Getting Started and the Boot-Up Process

Before we can begin to use Windows 8.1, we will need to be sure the computer is connected properly to the display, power, and any peripheral devices. In the following section we will take a look at the physical ports on a desktop and laptop, and make sure the correct cables are connected to the computer before powering on the PC.

Physical Ports on the PC

On the chart that follows, you will find the physical ports on many desktops and laptops, and the common uses for each port.

Figure 1.1: Desktop and Laptop Ports

Figure 1.2: Computer Ports

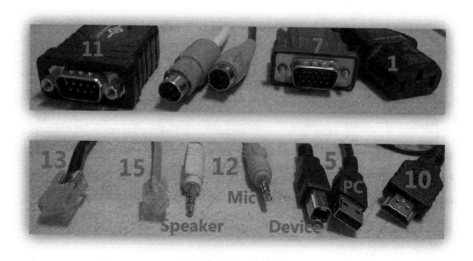

Figure 1.3: Computer Cables

1. **Desktop Power Connector** - This is the electrical power connector that plugs into your wall outlet.

2. **Laptop AC Adapter Power Connector** - This port will vary by brand and model, but connects to the AC power adapter that runs and charges the laptop.

3. **PS/2 Keyboard Connector** - This port (usually purple) is used only for a PS/2 type keyboard connector.

4. **PS/2 Mouse Connector** - This port (usually green) is used only for a PS/2 type mouse connector.

5. **USB Port** - This port is used by a large number of devices, from USB keyboards & mice, to printers, cameras, and mp3 players. The order that devices are plugged into these ports does not matter. Some devices may require drivers to be installed before a device can be recognized and used.

6. **Parallel Port** - This is a legacy connector that is no longer common on new PC's. In the past, it was primarily used as a connection to printers and scanners.

7. **VGA or D-Sub Video Port** - This is the most common video connector to an external monitor or TV. This is likely the connector that your monitor uses, and the connector has been common for many years.

8. **S-Video Port** - This video connector is rarely used to connect to an external display or TV, and lacks the video quality that other video connections provide.

9. **DVI Video Port** (varies by type) - There are several types of DVI ports and cables, and not all are compatible with each other. This video port is used to connect to an external monitor or TV.

10. **HDMI Video & Audio Port** - Many new systems include this all-in-one, high definition video & audio connector, used to output video & audio to an external monitor or TV.

11. **Serial Port** - This legacy port was used mainly to connect to older legacy hardware for communication. It is no longer common to find this connector on many desktops & laptops.

12. **Surround Sound Audio/Line-in/Speakers Out/Microphone Port** - The layout of the 1/8" audio jacks will vary, and depend upon stereo or surround sound output capabilities. On most PC's, there are three audio ports: Line-in (usually blue), Stereo Speaker Output (usually green), and Microphone In (usually pink).

13. **Ethernet Port** - This port looks like an oversized phone jack. An Ethernet cable plugs into this port for use with your high speed internet connection.

14. **Desktop Wireless Card Antenna** - The wireless card antenna connects to your wireless router to establish a high speed internet connection.

15. **Dial-up Modem** - This legacy port/card was used primarily for dial-up internet access in the past, but is rare now due to the ubiquity of high speed networks.

16. **1394/Firewire Port** - This port is not commonly found on current PC's, but was used as a data connector for video cameras and some peripheral devices.

17. **eSATA Port** - The eSATA port is an external serial ATA port used as a high speed connection to external hard drives and similar devices.

18. **PCMCIA Port, Laptop Expansion Ports** - Laptop expansion ports will vary depending on the age of the system, but these ports are primarily used for add-on cards. Add-on wireless cards and mobile broadband cards are one commonly used PCMCIA card.

19. **Card Reader Slots** - These ports vary on each system, and are only compatible with specific

types of cards. These ports allow you to plug in a camera memory card and access pictures stored on the device. Memory cards show up as a removable device in File Explorer.

20. **DisplayPort** - This port is usually used to output video and audio to a monitor or external display. DisplayPort has a similar functionality to HDMI, but is not compatible with HDMI without a specific adapter.

21. **SPDIF Out (Sony/Philips Digital Interconnect Format)** - This digital audio port is usually used to output sound to external audio equipment, such as a surround sound stereo receiver.

On a desktop PC we need to be sure that at least the keyboard, mouse, monitor video cable, and power for both the monitor and tower are all connected. You may also have speakers, an Ethernet cable, and other peripheral devices connected. On a laptop you will need the AC power adapter connected, as well as any peripheral devices you wish to use. We can proceed to the next section once the required cables are in place.

Powering On the Computer

To begin, we first need to power on the computer. While every computer will vary in design, generally the power button will tend to be on the front of a desktop tower or above the keyboard on an open laptop (Figure 1.4). Generally the power button may have a symbol with a circle and a line through it.

Once you have located the power button, give it a quick press to power on your system if it is not already powered on.

Figure 1.4: Desktop & Laptop Power Button

The first screen you may see will likely be the BIOS POST screen or a screen with the computer manufacturer's logo. Following that screen, you will likely see the Windows 8.1 splash screen with a spinning circle of dots showing that Windows is booting up.

First Boot Initial Setup

If this is the first time you are powering on your Windows 8.1 PC you will likely see the initial setup screens that follow. Each of these steps will configure settings on the computer and allow you to personalize the system with the settings you select.

The first screen you may encounter is the Enter Product Key screen. In most configurations the initial setup will not prompt for the product key, as it will usually be saved on the system hardware or entered earlier during a disc-based installation.

In the next screen, you will be prompted to choose your country/region, language, and keyboard layout. Click the Next button to continue after configuring your settings.

Next you will be required to accept the license terms to use Windows 8.1. If you agree to the license terms, check the "I Accept" checkbox, then the Accept button to proceed.

You should now see the Personalize screen. This screen has a theme color slide bar and a textbox for the PC name. Select your desired color theme and enter a name for your PC, then click Next.

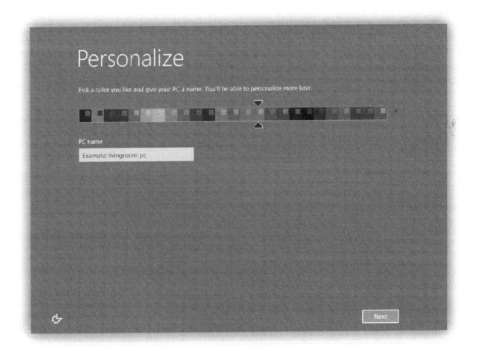

Figure 1.5: Personalize Your PC

After the Personalize screen, you will find the Settings screen with the options to Use Express Settings or to Customize. The express settings option will use the listed settings as the default.

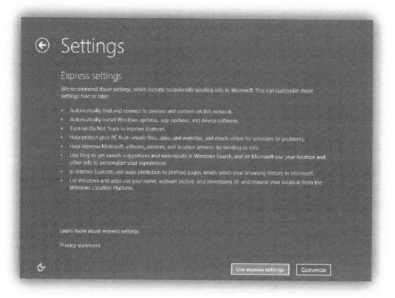

Figure 1.6: Settings Options Screen

 Select the Use Express Settings option for the preferred default settings.

You may be prompted to connect to a wireless network at this time if your PC is not already connected to the internet. You can select your WiFi hotspot and connect if you wish. You may be asked if you would like to automatically find and connect to devices on the same network. It is generally recommended to automatically connect to devices on a home or work network, but not on a public network where your data may be accessible to strangers.

Figure 1.7: Network Settings

Choosing the Customize option will display several screens for manually selecting system settings (Figure 1.8 – Figure 1.10). You can manually select the options you wish according to your own preferences.

The first settings screen will ask about automatically installing important security updates, updating device drivers, and updating apps. You can also enable SmartScreen and Do Not Track requests in Internet Explorer.

Figure 1.8: Settings Screen – Updates & Privacy

The next Settings page will deal with sharing your data with Microsoft and apps installed on the computer.

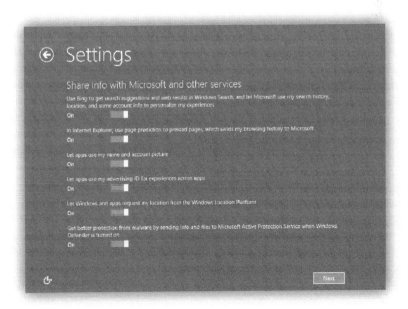

Figure 1.9: Send Data Reports

The last Settings page will deal with sending data to Microsoft to report problems with programs and web pages. You can also enable sending data to help Microsoft improve products and services.

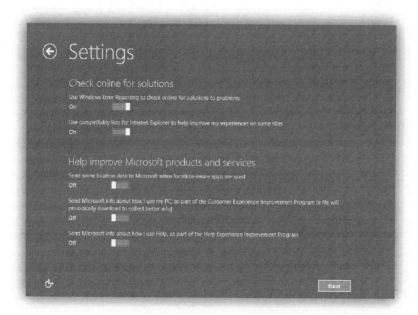

Figure 1.10: Solutions & Sharing

If your PC is already connected to the internet, you may see a screen prompting you to create a Microsoft Account or a local account. A Microsoft Account is a Microsoft hosted email address such as Hotmail or Outlook. Signing in with a Microsoft Account will allow you to sync your PC settings across multiple computers. I recommend that you use a local account unless you specifically require some of the features of a Microsoft Account. If you have a Microsoft Account and wish to use it, you can enter in on this page. To create a Microsoft Account or log in with a local account, click the Create A New Account link.

> To create a Local Account instead of a Microsoft Account, click the Create A New Account link. On the next screen click the Sign In Without A Microsoft Account link at the bottom of the page.

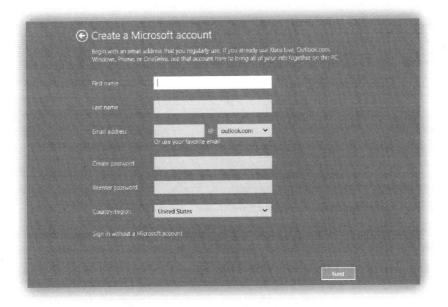

Figure 1.11: Microsoft Account Sign In

Enter the requested information to create a new Microsoft Account. To create a local account instead, simply click the Sign In Without A Microsoft Account link at the bottom of the page.

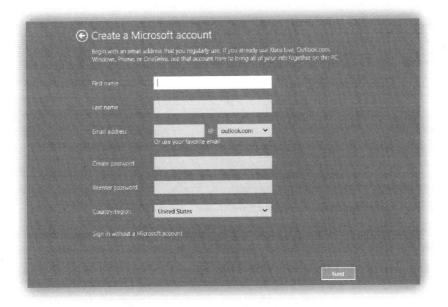

Figure 1.12: Create a Microsoft Account

Enter in a username and password (if desired) in the text fields. Click Finish to complete the initial setup process.

11

Figure 1.13: Create an Account Screen

After you create a user account the computer will finish the initial setup process and show a few brief instructions for using the PC. After this process you will then boot to either the Windows Desktop or the Start Screen.

Windows Login and Lock Screen

When you power on your Windows 8.1 PC, it may boot directly to the Start Screen, Windows Desktop, or to a Lock/Login screen. A lock screen is a wallpaper that displays the date and time and customizable information. It is usually displayed when you manually lock the PC or when it sits idle for a set period of time.

Figure 1.14: Windows 8.1 Lock Screen

Single left-click with your mouse to unlock the screen. Touch and slide up on the lock screen while using a touch screen device. If you see the Login screen with any user accounts on the PC, click the user account you wish to use. If there is a password for the account, you will be prompted to enter it.

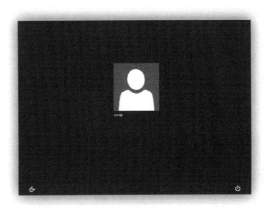

Figure 1.15: User Account Login Screen

If you only have a single user account and it does not have a password, then your PC will continue to boot up and immediately load the Start Screen or Windows Desktop.

Windows 8.1 with Update 1 is configured to boot to the Windows Desktop if a keyboard and mouse are present, or to the Start Screen if you are using a touch screen device instead. Now that the initial Windows 8.1 setup and configuration is complete, we can start learning and exploring the many new features in Windows 8.1.

If you are currently running Windows 8 instead of Windows 8.1, you can install the free Windows 8.1 update in the Windows Store on the Start Screen. Click on the green Windows Store tile to launch the app. If all of the Windows 8.1 prerequisites have been installed through Windows Update you will see a link to download Windows 8.1 when you first open the Windows Store. If the prerequisites have not been installed, take a look at the section on Windows Update in this book to learn how to download the required updates before downloading Windows 8.1.

Figure 1.16: Windows Store Update Tile

Click the Download button to begin downloading the Windows 8.1 update. This update is over three gigabytes large and will usually take at least an hour to download and install.

Figure 1.17: Windows 8.1 Download Details

After installing the Windows 8.1 update, be sure to check Windows Update for any additional updates that may need to be installed.

There have been some significant changes to this operating system when compared to previous versions. The Start Menu has been replaced, the Start Screen is now a primary user interface, and the OS has been redesigned for usability with a touch screen. In the sections that follow we will take a look at many of the components of Windows 8.1 and examine the many new features.

Chapter Review Questions:
1. Identify the ports on your computer and describe the purpose of each port.
2. What is one advantage on using a Microsoft Account instead on a Local Account on multiple Windows 8.1 computers you own?
3. What screen will you likely see when your touch screen tablet completes setup if you have a single user account without a password?

Chapter 2 - Windows 8.1 Primary Components

In Windows 8.1, there are three primary components to the operating system. They are the Windows Start Screen and Modern UI apps, the Charms Bar, and the Windows Desktop. In the following sections I will walk you through the different parts of the Windows Desktop, Charms Bar, and Start Screen, and provide an overview of how to use each feature.

Windows Start Screen

The Windows Start Screen is the successor to the Start Menu that was available in previous versions of Windows. The Start Screen contains tiles that are used to launch installed programs and apps. This interface is designed for ease of use on a touch screen monitor or tablet.

If the Start Screen is not currently open you can open it by clicking on the Start Button in the lower-left corner of the screen with your mouse. If you are using a tablet or touch screen device, you can open the Start Screen by swiping in from the right side of the screen with your finger in order to open the Charms Bar. Then click the Windows icon on the Charms Bar to open the Start Screen (see the section on the Charms Bar for more details). You can also click the Windows Key on your keyboard, or touch the home button on a tablet device.

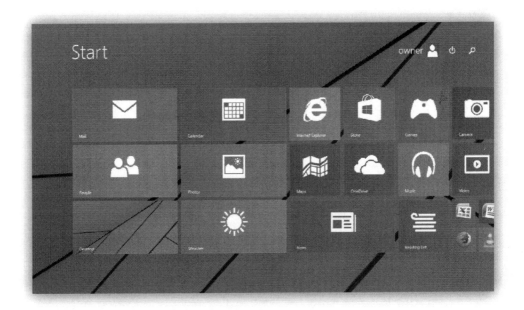

Figure 2.1: Windows Start Screen

If you right-click with your mouse on the Start Button in the lower-left corner of the Windows Desktop, you will see a context menu with links to various control panel items and administrative tasks, as seen in Figure 2.2.

15

Figure 2.2: Windows Start Button Right-click Options

To shut down your Windows 8.1 PC you can right-click the Start Button and select Shut Down Or Sign Out, then click the Shut Down option from the submenu. You can also use the Power icon on the Start Screen, or use the Settings Charm to shut down.

Next, we will look at how to use the Start Screen and Modern UI Apps.

Navigating and Customizing the Start Screen

On a touch device you can swipe left and right to scroll through the items on the Start Screen. With a mouse simply move the mouse towards the edge of the window, or use the wheel on your mouse, and the screen will scroll through the list. Pinch in or out on your touch screen to zoom on the Start Screen. You can also zoom by using either the scroll wheel on your mouse while holding the Ctrl key on your keyboard, or by clicking the zoom button in the lower right corner of the window.

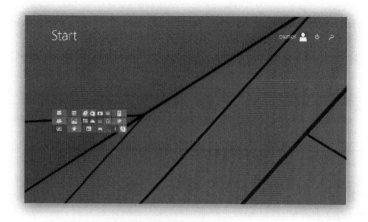

Figure 2.3: Start Screen Zoomed Out

Not all apps installed on the PC will be pinned to the Start Screen. To view all of the apps on the PC, left-click with your mouse on the small arrow in the lower left section of the Start Screen. On a touch screen you can swipe up from the bottom edge of the Start Screen or touch the small arrow icon to view all programs on the PC.

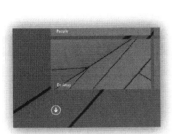 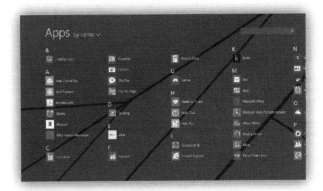

Figure 2.4: Start Screen View All Apps Arrow and All Apps Screen

Click the small arrow icon in the lower-left corner of the Start Screen to view all Apps. Swipe up from the bottom edge of a touch screen to view all Apps on a tablet.

Items pinned in the Start Screen often are live tiles that display content such as headlines, updates, and messages, without having to open the app. Tiles on the Start Screen can be rearranged, resized, and added/removed. Clicking on an app launches that program, while right-clicking will give options for the tile. On a touch screen, access the app commands for an app by touching and holding your finger on the desired app tile. Tile options include: unpin from the Start Screen, uninstall the program, make the tile larger or smaller, open program in a new window, open program with Administrative privileges, open the location of the linked file, and turn live tile on/off.

To rearrange the order of the tiles on the Start Screen, left-click and drag the tile you wish to move to the desired location. On a touch screen you can touch and hold the tile before dragging it to a new location. Move the tile to the desired location on the Start Screen and then release. Tap on a blank area of the Start Screen on a touch screen to end customization of the tiles.

Figure 2.5: Drag Tile to Desired Location

To move multiple tiles at the same time you can hold the Ctrl key on your keyboard and single left-click each tile with your mouse. After selecting all of the tiles you wish to move, click and drag them to the new desired location.

Figure 2.6: Select Multiple App Tiles

Right click a blank area of the Start Screen to see the Name Groups option. To name groups on a touch screen, swipe down on the screen to open the App Commands, and then tap Customize. Select the group you wish to name and type in a description for the group. To remove the group name text, click the "X" icon in the textbox.

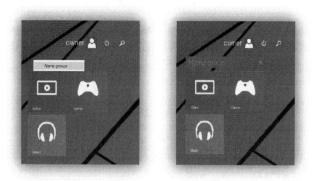

Figure 2.7: Name Groups Context Menu and Group Name Textbox

After the group has been named you can drag other tiles into that category for easier access. Now we are ready to pin our favorite apps to the Start Screen and Taskbar.

Pin Apps to the Start Screen and Taskbar

To pin an app on the Start Screen to the Taskbar, right click the tile or touch and hold the tile on a touch screen. Select the Pin To Taskbar option to pin the app.

Figure 2.8: Start Screen Tile Options

To pin an app from the All Apps Start Screen listing, right-click on the tile and select the Pin To Start option. On a touch screen device, touch and hold the tile. Then choose Pin To Start from the app command options. To view the traditional Windows Desktop you can click the Desktop tile on the Start Screen.

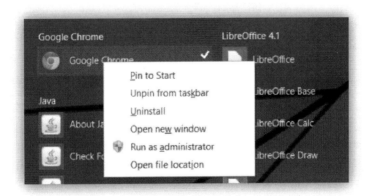

Figure 2.9: Start Screen All Apps Options

To pin a Windows Desktop application shortcut or executable file to the Start Screen, right-click the item and select Pin to Start. To pin the same item to the Windows Desktop taskbar you can right-click the item and select Pin to Taskbar. A webpage can be pinned to the Windows Desktop taskbar by dragging and releasing the Desktop Internet Explorer webpage tab down to the taskbar. For certain sites this allows the pinned site to act similar to an installed application. For instance, many webmail sites provide notifications to the pinned icon when new mail is received, and the jump list may reflect site specific tasks, such as Inbox and Compose New E-mail.

Figure 2.10: Pin Desktop Programs to the Start Screen

With Update 1 for Windows 8.1 you will notice a power button and search icon in the upper right corner of the Start Screen. These items will not appear if you are on a touch screen device without a keyboard and mouse attached. Clicking the power button icon will provide several shutdown options. The search button will launch the Search Charm – allowing you to search for files, apps, settings, or the web.

Figure 2.11: Start Screen Shutdown Menu

You will notice a Start Button when your mouse cursor into the lower left corner of the screen. Click this button to switch back to an open app or to open the Start Screen while in an app.

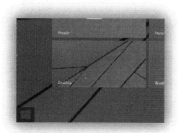

Figure 2.12: Start Button

When you move your cursor along the bottom of the Start Screen the Taskbar will appear. Pinned programs, open applications, and open Modern UI Apps will appear on the Taskbar.

Figure 2.13: Taskbar On The Start Screen

In the next section we will discuss settings that allow you to personalize your user account and PC.

User Account Personalization Options

While on the Start Screen, you can click on the user profile picture in the upper-right corner on the screen to select several actions. You can change your profile picture, sign out of the PC, switch to a different user, or lock the PC.

Figure 2.14: User Account Menu

Personalizing the Start Screen

In Windows 8.1 there are numerous ways to customize your Start Screen design and color. To adjust these settings, open the Settings charm while on the Start Screen, then click Personalize. You can choose from multiple background themes and choose the background and accent colors for the theme.

Figure 2.15: Start Screen Theme and Colors

21

Selecting the Tiles link under the Personalize option will allow you to show more apps in the Apps view and show Administrative Tools. You can also click the Clear button to remove personal information from tiles on the Start Screen.

Figure 2.16: Tile Options

Now that we are comfortable navigating and using the Start Screen, we will take a look at the next major component to Windows 8.1-the Charms Bar.

Charms Bar

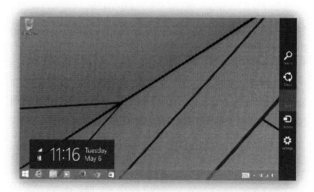

Figure 2.17: Desktop with Charms Bar Displayed

The Charms Bar is a new menu bar that runs along the right side of the screen. The Charms Bar with its five icons can be opened at any point regardless of the app that is open on the screen. This provides a consistent menu interface that doesn't interfere with the functionality of open applications. Hover your cursor in the upper or lower right corner of the screen to open the Charms Bar. On a touch screen you can swipe your finger in from the right edge to open the Charms Bar.

> Move your cursor to the upper-right or lower-right corner of the screen to open the Charms Bar. Swipe from the right edge of a touch screen to open the Charms Bar.

The Charms Bar offers 5 primary links: Search, Share, Start Screen, Devices, and Settings.

The **Search Charm** allows you to find a program, file, or setting that matches the search term. You can narrow results by clicking on the filter item below the search box. You can also click a specific app and search within that app, such as searching for a specific e-mail in the mail app or a specific town in the weather app.

The **Share Charm** can share the current app content with another app or person. For instance, if you want to share a website you are viewing on the Internet Explorer app with someone via e-mail, you can click the share Charms Bar link, and click Mail.

The **Start** Screen link opens the Start Screen. If you are already on the Start Screen, this link will open the last app you were using.

The **Devices Charm** link can be used to connect to various hardware peripherals. You can use this option to print from within an app, connect to an external display, stream video to a device, or to sync devices.

The **Settings Charm** allows you to view common settings, such as network status and volume level, and provides options for changing app and PC settings. App settings will vary depending on the running app. They will allow you to change settings that are unique to that running program. On the Desktop, the Settings option provides links to the desktop control panel, personalization options, and PC information. The Change PC Settings link at the bottom of the Settings sidebar opens the Modern UI Control Panel. The Modern UI Control Panel changes system wide options, such as personalization (lock screen, start screen, account picture), privacy options, and update settings.

Search Charm

The Search Charm can be used to search within an app, or from the Start Screen as in Figure 2.18. You can filter results by selecting the relevant filter beneath from the dropdown box next to the word "Everywhere", or search within a specific app.

Figure 2.18: Search Charm

If you don't click on a specific app, file, or setting, you can click the search button to launch the Search app. The left pane of this app will list any matching files, settings, or apps. The right pane will list various Bing web search results.

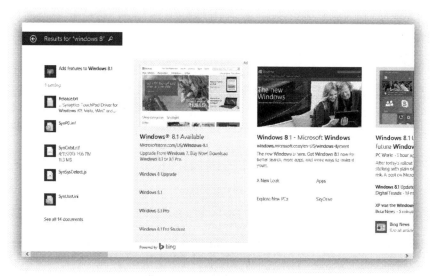

Figure 2.19: Bing Search Results

Left-click a Bing web search result to open the page in a browser window. Right-click a search result to select Copy Link from the App Commands. You can then paste the link into another program.

Share Charm

In the Figure 2.20 you can see the Share Charm open in the Modern UI Internet Explorer app. The options currently displayed allow the webpage link to be shared with either the Mail app or the People App. Depending on the app that is open and the Share-enabled apps installed, other Share results may appear in the list.

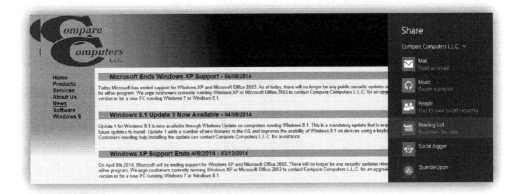

Figure 2.20: Share Charm

Devices Charm

The devices charm will list printers and other devices available that support the feature. You can also stream to a supported TV, sync with other hardware, and access wired and wireless hardware devices via the Play option. The Print link will allow you to print the selected page or text to an available printer. The Project option is used to configure the display for use with a projector or external screen. You can duplicate the display so the both screens show the same image, use only one of the two displays, or extend the display so that the output is extended onto the secondary monitor.

Figure 2.21: Devices Charm, Print To Device, and Project To Device

Settings Charm

The Settings Charm will allow you to configure app specific settings, system settings, and shutdown options. You can also view notifications, connect to networks, and configure audio and display settings from the Settings Charm.

Figure 2.22: Settings Charm

To shut down your PC, click the Settings charm, then the Power option. You can then choose if you would like to shut down, restart, or sleep.

Figure 2.23: Settings Charm Shutdown Options

Now that we have explored the new Charms Bar features, let's take a look at a more familiar component of Windows-the Windows Desktop.

Windows Desktop

The Windows Desktop is the traditional interface for working with files and desktop applications. The Windows 8.1 Desktop is similar to the desktop that was available in Windows 7 - with some minor changes.

With the Start Screen open, click the Desktop link to open the traditional desktop. You will notice several main components on the screen while looking at the Windows desktop. Desktop icons for programs, files, and folders are located on top of the background wallpaper image. The second main component is the taskbar that usually runs along the bottom of the screen.

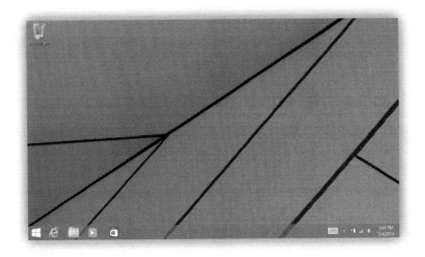

Figure 2.24: Windows Desktop and Taskbar

To search for a file, program, or setting, simply start typing the name of a program, file, or option while the Start Screen is open and you will find a list of results appear as you type. You can then click the item you wish to use, thereby quickly accessing that resource.

Windows Taskbar

In the lower left corner of the Windows Desktop there are usually several programs pinned to the taskbar. Usually you will have at least the taskbar links shown in Figure 2.25, but other programs may be pinned to the taskbar as well.

Figure 2.25: Default Items on the Windows Taskbar

By default, the first item to the right of the Start Button is Internet Explorer. This web browser can be used to view websites and access internet resources. To the right of this item is File Explorer. File Explorer is a file manager that is used to view files, folders, and drives that are accessible to your system. Icons to the right of File Explorer will vary from system to system. Icons on the taskbar can be added, removed, and sorted any time you choose.

When you right-click on programs pinned to the taskbar, you will see what is known as a Jump List. A Jump List provides quick access to common features or files, and allows items to be pinned to the list. The jump list for Internet Explorer will list frequently visited websites or sites that you have pinned for faster accessibility. The jump list for Microsoft Word will list recently opened documents and any documents that you have manually pinned. To pin an item to the jump list, open the jump list and click the thumbtack icon next to the listed filename.

Figure 2.26: Jump Lists

Tip! Pin commonly used files to the Jump List by pressing the thumbtack icon next to the filename in the Jump List.

When you have a window open, hovering your cursor over the taskbar icon for that window will display a thumbnail image. This makes it easier to view the open windows you want to access while you have multiple windows and applications running at the same time.

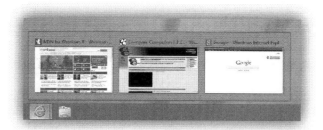

Figure 2.27: Live Preview Thumbnail

The desktop area is the area on top of your background wallpaper where icons, folders, and files can be located. Many programs place a shortcut on the desktop during their installation in order to make it easier to run the application. You can save files to the desktop, but I recommend grouping files by type (images, music, videos) in their respective folders located in File Explorer for consistency. Many programs will look for specific files in those folders – for instance, Windows Media Player will search your Music folder for any audio files, and will automatically import the songs into the program, making them available for listening all in one place.

It can be difficult managing multiple program windows that are open at the same time. There are a few options available for easily accessing the specific window that you want to work with. On the far right corner of the taskbar is a thin bar icon called Show Desktop. If you hover over this icon all windows on the screen will minimize until you move the cursor off of the icon.

This feature is known as Windows Peek. If you click Show Desktop, it will minimize all windows, even if you move your cursor off of the icon. By clicking it again, you can restore all previously minimized windows to the way they were.

Figure 2.28: Show Desktop Icon

To the left of the Show Desktop icon on the taskbar, the notification area is where some background programs and alerts will appear. Windows 8.1 has made improvements to the notification area in an attempt to make it not interfere with normal everyday tasks. In previous versions of Windows, pop up alerts in this area lead to distractions and other problems. With Windows 8.1 the majority of those issues have been resolved. The Action Center now handles many of the critical alerts relating to system security and maintenance. When issues need to be resolved, the Action Center will alert you with a flag with a red circle and "X", along with an alert balloon. Clicking on the balloon or Action Center icon will provide you with more information on the issue and how to resolve the problem.

Figure 2.29: Notification Area and Action Center

Taskbar Properties

Settings for the look and behavior of the Taskbar are configured in the Taskbar And Navigation Properties window. This feature also lets you change whether the PC boots to the Desktop or Start Screen when you log in, as well as other Start Screen navigation settings. To change these settings simply right-click on the Taskbar and select Properties.

The Taskbar tab will provide options for locking the Taskbar to its current position, hiding the Taskbar, and settings its location on the screen. You can also adjust the size of buttons on the Taskbar. Now that Windows Store apps appear on the taskbar you can easily navigate between the Desktop and full screen apps with a simple click.

In the Navigation tab you will see options for enabling or disabling the corner navigation areas. You can disable the upper-right Charms corner and upper-left corner listing recent apps. The first checkbox in the Start Screen section allows you to go directly to the Desktop when you boot up or close all Modern UI Apps on the screen. The option to show your Desktop background on the Start Screen makes for a less jarring transition between the two screens. The Show Start On The Display I'm Using option makes working on a multi-monitor setup easier by displaying the Start Screen when you need it on the screen you are actively working in. The Apps View option displays all apps instead of the larger Start Screen tiles when you go to the Start Screen. Listing Desktop apps first will sort them to the front of the Start Screen Apps View list.

Figure 2.30: Taskbar Properties and Navigation Options

> The Navigation tab in the Taskbar And Navigation Properties window can be used to make the PC boot directly to the Windows Desktop instead of the Start Screen.

The Jump Lists tab lets you adjust the number of recent items stored in each Jump List. You can enable or disable the storing of recently opened programs and items in Jump Lists. The Toolbars tab is used to add additional toolbars to the Taskbar. The most commonly enabled option is the Touch Keyboard for use on touch screen devices.

Figure 2.31: Jump List Properties and Toolbar Properties

Desktop Window Management

If you are working with two windows and wish to easily resize them so they both occupy half of the screen, Windows 8.1 has an easy to use feature called Windows Snap. Windows snap allows you to drag the title bar (very top of program window) of one program to one side of the screen edge to automatically resize the program to half of the screen. Dragging the other program's title bar to the opposite side of the screen edge resizes it to the other half of the screen. This feature makes it handy to read information on one screen and type in the other window, without having to minimize either screen.

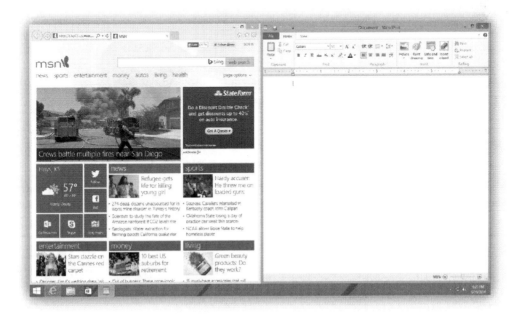

Figure 2.32: Windows Snap

Window Shake is a Windows 8.1 feature that allows you minimize all windows except the one you want to work with. Simply click and hold the title bar of the open program you want to work with, and shake your cursor on the screen. All other windows will minimize. If you repeat the process, all windows will restore back again.

A simple keyboard key combination is another option for easily moving between open windows. On your keyboard, hold down the Alt key (usually located next to the spacebar on your keyboard). Then click the Tab key on your keyboard. You should see a window that displays all of the open program windows on your computer. By continuing to hold the Alt key, and tapping the Tab key, you can cycle through the open programs. Release the Alt key to select the window you wish to open.

To change your desktop wallpaper, theme, screen saver, and other options, right-click on a blank area of the desktop and click Personalize. This will open the personalization section of the control panel. Clicking the four items at the bottom of the window (Desktop Background, Window Color, Sounds, and Screen Saver) will allow you to adjust those settings. In the Desktop Background section, you can select multiple images that will cycle through as the wallpaper at the selected interval.

In Chapter 3, we will explore the Windows Desktop in more detail by learning about traditional desktop applications and their interfaces.

Chapter Review Questions:
1. What are the three primary components in Windows 8.1?
2. Name three ways to safely shut down a PC running Windows 8.1 Update 1.
3. How do you change to computer to boot to the Windows Desktop instead of the Start Screen?
4. Describe how you can quickly open a file with the Jump List feature.
5. How do you unpin a program from the Taskbar?
6. What are some of the notifications you may see in the Action Center?
7. How would you quickly device two windows so they are side-by-side on the screen?

Chapter 3 - Exploring Desktop Application Windows & File Explorer

Application Interfaces

Every application window layout will vary depending on how it was designed. However, many applications have similarities in their design and layout, which we will review in the following section.

Figure 3.1: Application Window Layout

The title bar is the uppermost portion of an application window that usually contains the name of the running application. To the right of the title bar in the upper right corner of the window, you will usually find three icons: a bar, a box, and an "X". The bar icon on the left is the minimize button, which will keep the window open, but minimize it to the taskbar. The middle square icon is the maximize/restore button. Clicking it will either maximize the window to full screen, or restore it to a smaller size on the screen. The "X" icon on the far right is the close button. Clicking this button will exit the current application or window.

Beneath the Minimize, Maximize, and Close buttons on some application windows, you may find a search box. This search box allows you to search for files, folders, and settings within the current window. There may be an address bar to the left of the search box in some windows. The address bar may show the current page, website, folder, or other location that you are currently accessing.

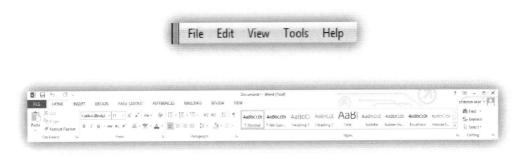

Figure 3.2: Menu Bar & Ribbon Bar

Below the title bar many programs also have a menu bar or ribbon user interface. The menu bar contains drop down menus that perform actions for that program. Usually you will find drop down menus for File, Edit, View, Tools, and Help. The menu bar generally contains options for creating and opening files, saving files, printing, editing, and configuring layout. Programs using the ribbon user interface, such as File Explorer and Microsoft Office 2007, 2010, and 2013, are becoming more commonplace. Ribbon UI's offer a clear visual representation of various functions and tend to be more touch-friendly on touch screen monitors. Ribbon UI's have tabs, similar to the tabs on a paper file folder. Under each tab are icons for functions relevant to that tab.

Next we will look at File Explorer-the file management tool in Windows 8.1.

File Explorer

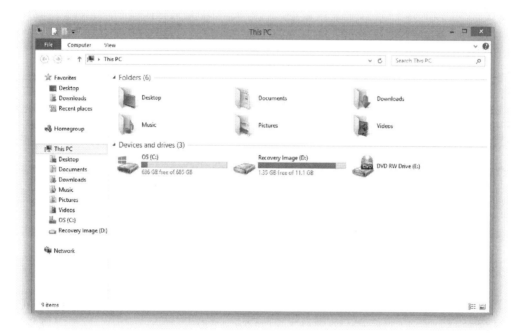

Figure 3.3: File Explorer Layout

By default, the File Explorer program window will have a title bar, address bar, and search box. The Minimize, Maximize, and Close buttons will be located in the upper-right corner of the window. The Ribbon Interface will expand to show available options when one of the ribbon tabs is clicked. Below the address bar are six sections to the main window: the Ribbon UI menu bar, the navigation pane, the library pane, the details pane, the preview pane (disabled by default), and the file list.

From the Home tab you can copy, paste, move, and delete files and folders. You can create a new folder or item, view properties for selected items, and easily access options for selecting files.

Figure 3.4: Expanded Ribbon UI Home Tab

In the File Explorer Share tab you can e-mail, compress, burn, print, and fax files and folders. You can configure sharing and security options for the selected file or folder.

Figure 3.5: File Explorer Share Tab

The File Explorer View tab is used to configure the onscreen layout of the window panes, change the icon size, sort files, and change view options for the system.

Figure 3.6: File Explorer View Tab

The Ribbon UI menu bar's contents will change depending on the files selected and the contents of the currently open folder. Some of the options in the Ribbon UI menu bar allow you to organize and change the layout onscreen, share files, create new folders, and burn files to disc, among other features. The navigation pane provides quick shortcuts to folders, drives, libraries, and network paths. The library pane displays information about the currently open library, and has a link to view, add, or remove library folders locations. The details pane displays details of the currently selected file, folder, or drive, such as size, sharing status, modification date, and creation date. The preview pane (when enabled) allows you to view a preview of selected documents and other supported files, without having to open the file. Supported audio files can be played directly from the preview pane without needing to open a media player program.

The file list is the main section of the File Explorer window. It lists the file and folder names of objects in the current path. You can adjust the size of the icons in the file list by clicking on the View tab and choosing one of the layout options.

When you open File Explorer, usually you will see the Favorites, HomeGroup, This PC, and Network links on the left pane. Below you will find some basic information on these links and some other common file paths.

- **Favorites Folder** – Users can add commonly used folders to this list so that they show up in File Explorer favorites list.
- **Documents Folder** – This link takes you directly to the current user's documents folder. This folder generally contains only documents (such as Word documents, Excel spreadsheets, and other data files saved there), and not pictures, music, or other files.
- **Pictures Folder** – This link takes you directly to the current user's pictures folder. This folder generally contains only images (such as photos and saved pictures), and not documents, music, or other files.
- **Music Folder** – This link takes you directly to the current user's music folder. This folder generally contains only audio files (such as mp3's, wma's, and other audio types), and not documents, pictures, or other files.
- **This PC** – The computer link opens a File Explorer window showing the drives in your computer, such as "C:\" or Local Disk, DVD+/-RW DVD Burners, USB Storage Devices, Camera Cards, and other storage devices. Double-clicking on available drives will open the drive, allowing you to explore the contents and files.
- **Network** – This link allows access to any shared network folders and networked computers.
- **User Profile Folder** – This folder's name will vary depending on the account name that was created when the computer was first set up. It may be your own name, it may be "owner", or it could be something arbitrary – the main point being that when you click it, it takes you to the folder where the majority of your files (documents, pictures, music, etc.) all reside. Typically the path to the user profile folder is in "C:\Users\".

In chapter 4 we will briefly look at the file system in Windows 8.1. We will also review how to work with files and folders.

Chapter Review Questions:
1. Name three programs that use a Ribbon UI interface instead of a drop-down menu.
2. Which File Explorer tab allows you to Cut, Copy, and Paste?

Chapter 4 - Getting to Know the File System

Drives, Partitions, Folders, and files

When you open the This PC link in File Explorer, you will see a listing of the drives on your computer. Usually this will include at least your system drive (usually "C :\"), and an optical drive (usually your DVD Burner "D :\"). Your hard disk is the physical hard drive inside your computer where your data is stored. This drive may be divided into multiple partitions, which may appear as separate drives in File Explorer, even though they are stored on the same physical device. When you double-click on the system drive ("C :\") you will find a number of files and folders. To keep the concepts of drives, folders, and files straight, think of a filing cabinet. The cabinet is like a drive. The paper folder is like a folder on the drive. Each folder contains files. These files may be documents, music, pictures, or other types of data. To create a new folder, right-click in a blank space in the file list area, and choose New, then Folder. You can then type the name that you would like to use for the folder, followed by the Enter key on your keyboard. The folder will then be renamed.

Cut, Copy, Paste, and Delete

There are many ways to copy and paste files: keyboard shortcuts ("ctrl + c", "ctrl + v"), dragging and dropping the file, using menus ("File Menu – Edit – Copy/ Paste"), and right-clicking the file and choosing Copy or Paste. Usually the easiest method for most people to start with is to right-click on the file you wish to copy and click Copy from the context menu. To copy multiple files in the same location you can hold the "ctrl" key and left-click on the files you want to select. When your selection is complete you can right-click on one of the selected files and choose Copy from the context menu. Browse File Explorer to the destination path you desire, right-click in a blank area of the file list, and choose Paste from the context menu. To delete a file, right-click the file name, and choose Delete from the context menu. Confirm the file delete confirmation window if you are certain you wish to move the item to the recycle bin.

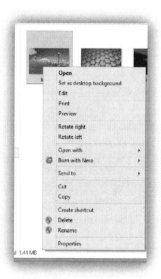

Figure 4.1: File Right-click Context Menu

Right-clicking on a file or folder allows you to Cut, Copy, or Delete. Right-clicking on a folder or blank area in Windows Explorer allows you to paste copied files.

Now that we have reviewed working with files and folders, we will turn our focus to working with some of the new apps available for Windows 8.1. In Chapter 5 we will learn how to use and configure settings for Modern UI Apps in Windows 8.1.

Chapter Review Questions:

1. Describe the differences between a drive, a partition, a folder, and a file.
2. Describe three different ways to copy and paste a file into a folder.

Chapter 5 - Modern UI and Windows Store Apps

The Windows Start Screen app layout and design is also known as Modern UI. Modern UI is designed to be easily used with a touch screen and to be fast, fluid, and simple. Configuration options and menus are hidden from view, leaving the entire screen for viewing content. In the following sections we will look at working with the full screen apps and how to configure their options.

In Figure 5.1 and 5.2, you can see how to use the sides and hot corners in Windows 8.1. Swipe in from the left edge on a touch screen to switch between active apps. Swipe in from the right edge on a touch screen to open the Charms Bar.

Figure 5.1: Touch Screen Gestures

With a mouse you can access active apps in the upper-left corner, open the Start Screen in the lower-left corner, and open the Charms Bar in the upper or lower right corners.

Figure 5.2: Mouse Hot Corners

Figure 5.3 provides information on accessing a Modern UI App's App Commands. Swipe from the top edge to open an app's App Commands.

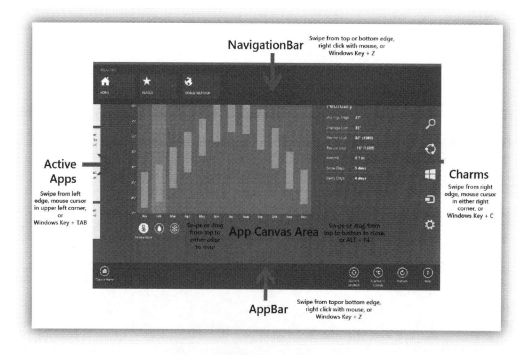

Figure 5.3: Modern UI App Navigation

App Commands

To navigate in an app and bring up menu command options, such as an address bar or play buttons, simply swipe from the top of the screen on a touch screen or right-click with a mouse to open a command. To select a specific item onscreen, like a photo or tile, swipe down or press and hold on the item with a touch screen. While using a mouse you can right-click the item with your mouse to select it. You can then choose the menu option for the desired action. App Commands consist of the NavigationBar located at the top of the screen and the AppBar located at the bottom of the screen. However, not all apps have both App Command bars.

In Figure 5.4 you will see the Modern UI Internet Explorer with the NavigationBar and AppBar open. From these menus in Internet Explorer, you can navigate between open tabs and enter in addresses into the AppBar's web address textbox.

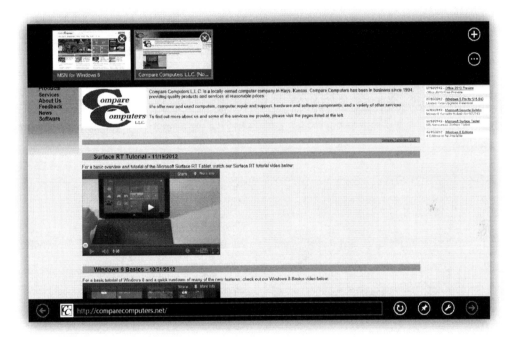

Figure 5.4: App Commands

App Window Management

Opening an app is as easy as selecting the tile for the app on the Start Screen. In the sections that follow, we will go over switching between multiple apps, closing apps, and working with multiple apps onscreen at the same time.

Active Apps

On a touch screen you can switch between active apps by swiping from the left edge to cycle through apps. You can cycle between active apps with a mouse by clicking the upper left corner of the screen.

41

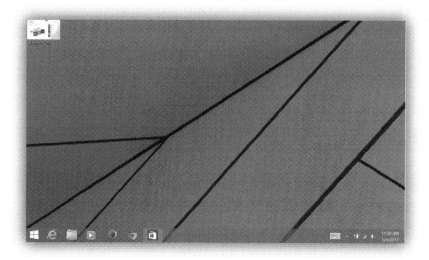

Figure 5.5: Switch Between Apps

To view all recent apps, swipe your finger from the left then back to the edge of the screen without lifting your finger. Then choose the program you wish to switch to. Move your mouse cursor to the upper left corner and then down to view all recent apps while using a mouse. Choose the program you wish to open. To close one of the items in the list you can right-click the item and choose Close.

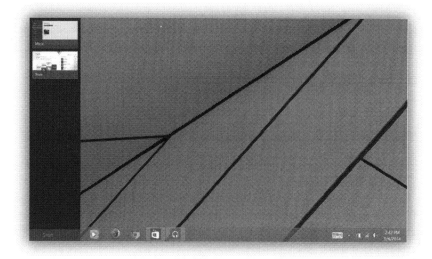

Figure 5.6: Active Apps/Close Apps

Modern UI Apps will have a Title Bar in Windows 8.1 when you move your cursor to the top of the app. Clicking on the program icon in the upper-left corner of a Modern UI App lets you split the app to the left or right side of the screen and minimize or close the app. You can also minimize or close the app my clicking the Minimize and Close buttons on the right side of the app's title bar.

Figure 5.7: App Title Bar Context Menu

Close An App

To close the app currently on the screen you can drag your mouse cursor or finger from the very top of the screen to the very bottom of the screen. You will see an animation as you perform the action of dragging the window to the bottom of the screen. You can also click the Close button in the upper-right corner of the app's title bar or right-click the app's taskbar icon and choose Close.

Snap An App

To use two apps at the same time, swipe your finger from the left and drag the recent app to either the right or left side. Wait until an area is available to drop the app into, then release. You can also click the Split Left or Split Right options from the app's title bar menu.

Figure 5.8: Snap An App

Dragging an open app from the top-center to the side edge will also snap an app. To use two apps at the same time with a mouse, view recent apps by moving your cursor to the upper left corner and moving down. Select the app you wish to use and drag it out, then back towards the side. Wait until an area is available to drop the app into, then release. Please note that your screen resolution must be at least 1366 x 768 in order to use the snap an app feature.

43

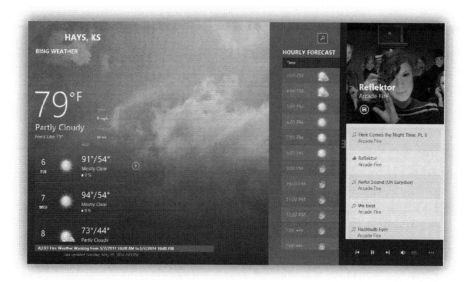

Figure 5.9: Expand Snap An App

To expand the snapped app and allow it to use more space on the screen, drag the app divider bar more to the right until it snaps in place.

Signing into Modern UI Apps with a Microsoft Account

When you first launch some Modern UI Apps, you may be prompted to sign in with a Microsoft Account. You can choose to migrate your local account into a Microsoft Account or sign into each app separately. Click the Next button to change your local account to a Microsoft Account, otherwise click the small text link that says Sign Into Each App Separately.

Figure 5.10: App Prompting For A Microsoft Account

You will be prompted to enter your Microsoft Account credentials. Click Save to sign into the individual app with your Microsoft Account.

Figure 5.11: Sign Into A Microsoft Account

In the following sections we will explore many of the built-in apps available in Windows 8.1.

Mail App

The Windows 8.1 Mail App is the default mail client built-in with Windows 8.1. Being a Modern UI App, it runs full screen with minimal menus and options in the way of the core program features. This mail client is designed to be ideal for a tablet or touch screen interface while still retaining a familiar design layout from previous Microsoft mail clients.

Mail Layout

The left pane of the app contains one or more e-mail accounts along with the folders for each account. Clicking on one of the folders displays that folder's list of e-mails, and previews the e-mail's text in the right pane. In Figure 5.12, the Inbox folder is open, with the first e-mail in the Inbox selected in the middle pane. The e-mail is displayed in the right pane. To start a new e-mail you can click the "+" sign in the upper-right corner of the window. To reply to the displayed e-mail, click the envelope with a back arrow that is located next to the plus sign. To delete the displayed e-mail, click the trash can icon to the right of the plus and reply icons.

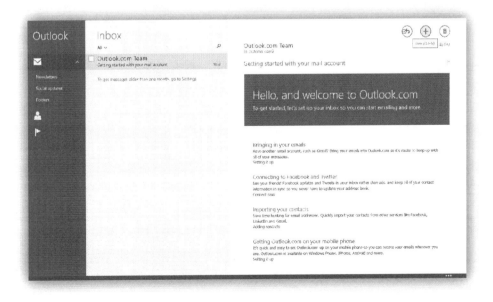

Figure 5.12: Mail App Inbox

45

After clicking the Compose New Mail button (plus sign), you will view the following screen (Figure 5.13). On the left you will find the "To:" and carbon copy sections (Cc), where you can type in a name or e-mail address, or click the plus key next to each textbox to select the address from your contacts. In the right pane you will see an area for the e-mail subject at the top, with an area for the e-mail message below that. To send the e-mail message when you are done, click the send mail button (the envelope icon in upper-right corner). If you wish to discard the message and not send it, click the trash can icon in the upper right corner.

Figure 5.13: Compose New Message Window

To view more sending options you can click the Show More link in the left pane. This will expand out the section to show an area for a blind carbon copy and for setting the message priority flag.

Click the paper clip icon in the upper-right corner to attach a file or picture to your email message. You will be able to browse for a file to attach to the email from one of the locations on the PC. You can also click the down-arrow icon next to the This PC text to select locations on the network or Cloud.

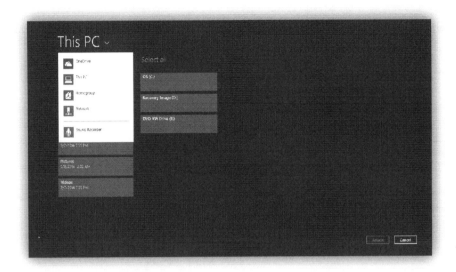

Figure 5.14: Browse Locations For Files To Attach

Browse and select the files you wish to attach, then click the Attach button.

Figure 5.15: Select Files To Attach

When you select the Folders link in the left pane of the Mail App, a list of folders will expand to the right. This lets you view emails located in the Inbox, Sent folder, and other locations.

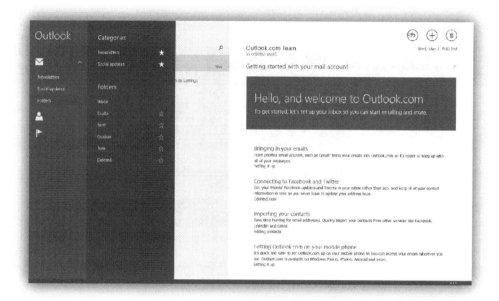

Figure 5.16: Mail Folders

To delete messages in the email list click the trash can icon in the list, the trash can icon in the upper-right corner of the preview pane, or check the checkbox of each message you want to remove and click delete on the keyboard or App Commands.

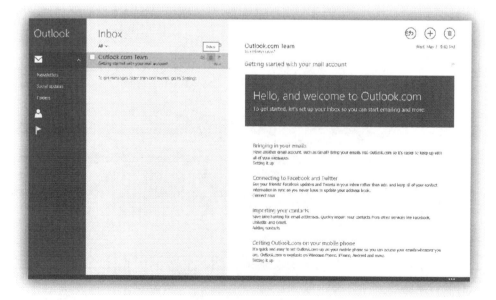

Figure 5.17: Delete Email Messages

Other options in the App Commands allow you to move messages to other folders, create and manage folders, mark messages as junk, and print messages.

Figure 5.18: Mail App Commands

Double clicking a message in the message list will open it in a new window. This window can be opened full screen or snapped to the side.

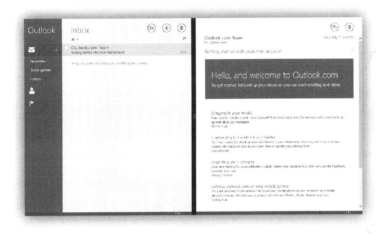

Figure 5.19: Read Message In A New Window

Selecting People from the left pane will allow you to browse and add contacts from the People App. Select the contact you wish to add as a favorite and they will be added to the list.

Figure 5.20: Saved Contacts In People Section

Next, we will look at configuring options for the Mail app and setting up an account for use with the program.

Mail Settings

By default, when you send several e-mails to the same contact, Mail will group these back-and-forth e-mails together as a Conversation and not in chronological order with the other e-mails received. To change this option open the Settings Charm and select the Options link. This screen will then allow you to switch off the conversations feature.

Figure 5.21: Disable Conversations Feature

Mail Account Setup

On first use you will need to add an account to the Mail App in order to receive e-mails. If you wish to add additional e-mail accounts, you can follow the same steps below. Start by opening the Settings Charm and click Accounts. Next click the Add An Account link. If the account you are setting up is provided by one of the listed services, you can select that service to use the preconfigured settings for your e-mail servers. Click Other Account from the list if your provider is not listed.

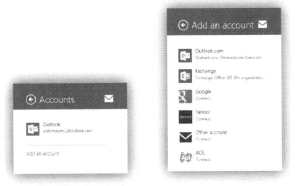

Figure 5.22: Account Options and Add an E-mail Account List

With many e-mail accounts you will want to select IMAP from the account type list. Check with your email provider for the account settings and mail servers you should use.

Figure 5.23: Manually Set Up an Account via Other Account

Enter your e-mail settings and mail server settings in the textboxes shown. When your settings match those provided by your e-mail provider, click the Connect button.

Figure 5.24: Manual Server Settings

51

To configure account settings for an e-mail account already set up in the Mail App, open the Settings Charm, then click Accounts. Select the account you wish to modify. If no accounts are listed you will need to click the Add An Account link and follow the steps above. The Account Settings screen allows you to configure various sync and notification settings for the desired account. From here you can determine how far back messages are to be downloaded and how often the PC checks for new messages. You can adjust notifications for incoming mail and disable or change message signatures.

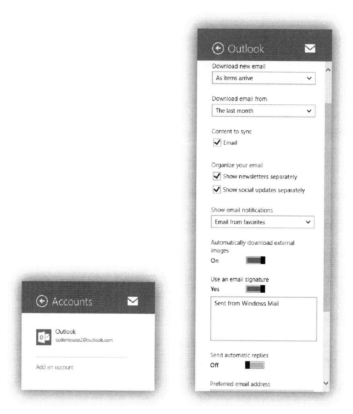

Figure 5.25: Account Options and Account Settings

The Mail app makes it easy to manage multiple e-mail accounts in one program. You can use the People app in Windows 8.1 to manage contacts from multiple social networks.

People App

The People App included in Windows 8.1 is an application to centralize and manage contacts from various social media services and e-mail providers. Contacts can be automatically imported by signing in with your Facebook, Twitter, or other social media login, or you can manually enter new contacts into the program. Once a social media account is linked with the app, you can see status updates from contacts, all in a single centralized app.

In the left pane you will find the option to connect to any social media accounts you may have when you first open the People App.

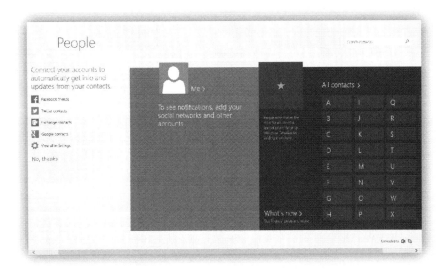

Figure 5.26: People App Initial Screen

The App Commands will provide you with links to navigate to Home, your profile, What's New, and All Contacts. You can also add a new contact by clicking the New Contact icon on the App Commands bar.

Figure 5.27: People App Commands

When you add a new contact you will be prompted for the account type that they will be linked to, along with the individual's contact information. Enter the contact's information and click the Save button to proceed.

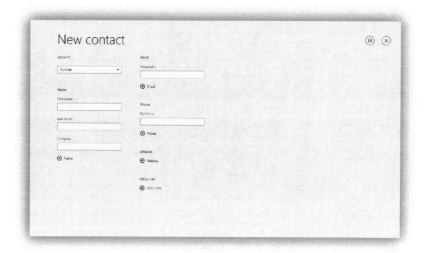

Figure 5.28: Add A New Contact

By selecting a contact from your list you can view basic information you have entered or they have made public. Click the links to Call, E-mail, Message, or Map the selected contact, or click More Info to view additional information.

Figure 5.29: Contact Details

Click the Favorite Star icon on a contact's main page to add the selected contact to your favorites list. Once added to your favorites list they will appear on the People App main screen.

You can view any social network accounts that you have set up by clicking Accounts under the Settings Charm. Click Add An Account to link with a social media service. From here you can select any of the listed services you use and import contacts into the app.

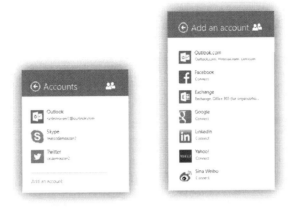

Figure 5.30: Account Settings and Add an Account Screens

In Figure 5.31, you can see that we have added a Twitter account to the People App, and can now view all of the Twitter users we are following as contacts.

Figure 5.31: Imported Twitter Contacts

Clicking on one of the Twitter contacts will show basic profile information and several recent tweets. You can choose to view the profile information, map location, and view all tweets from that contact as well.

Figure 5.32: Twitter Contact Information

You can scroll through the tweets from the selected contact under the What's New section. You can also click on the What's New link on the People App main page to view recent tweets by the contacts you are following on twitter.

Figure 5.33: What's New

To access friends and family from anywhere online, you can use the Skype App for instant messaging and video chats.

Skype

Skype™ is an instant messaging program that can also be used for voice and video calls to other computers and devices. The service can be used to make calls to an actual phone number for a charge. To use Skype, launch the Skype app and sign in with a free Skype Account or Microsoft Account.

Figure 5.34: Skype Main Window

After signing in you will see the Skype main window. The left-pane will list your recent activity. Your Skype contacts are located under the People section. Contacts will be sorted by their online status and name.

To change your availability status, account, or to sign out of the program, click the User icon in the upper-right corner of the Skype App. Changing your status will help your contacts to know when you are available to chat.

Figure 5.35: User Account Window

Right-click or swipe down on a touch screen to open the Skype App Commands. From this menu you can save a phone number and add a new contact.

Figure 5.36: Skype App Commands

Clicking the New Contact button allows you to search for a contact with a Skype name or email address that matches the search text entered.

Figure 5.37: Search For Contact

Select the user with the matching username or email address. Click the Add To Contacts button to send a friend request.

Figure 5.38: Add User To Contacts

You can choose to type a message to the individual so they know who is asking to become a contact. Click the Send button once you have typed the message.

Figure 5.39: Contact Request Message

Once someone has accepted your request, they will appear in your contacts list. Select the contact to start an instant message chat or video chat with them. Typing in the text box at the bottom of the screen will send the contact an instant message. To start a video chat, click the video camera icon. Click the phone receiver icon to begin a voice chat. The "+" icon provides options for sharing files, sending a video message, and adding other participants to a shared session.

Figure 5.40: Contact Chat Window

While chatting with a contact, you can right click or swipe from the top edge of a touch screen to open the App Commands. From the bottom App Commands window you can mark a contact as a favorite, view the contact's profile, and block or remove a contact.

Figure 5.41: Chat App Commands

When you click the video chat button Skype will attempt to reach the other person. They can choose to answer with video or with voice only, or choose to not answer the call. If they connect to the video chat you will see them full screen on your PC, with a thumbnail of what your own webcam sees in the lower right corner. In the video chat, the four icons at the bottom of the screen allow you to enable/ disable video, mute your microphone, and end the call. Clicking the "+" icon allows you to send an instant message, access the dial pad, add others to the chat, and share files.

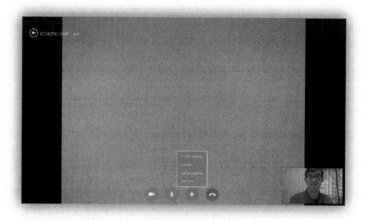

Figure 5.42: Video Call Window

If someone attempts to start a voice call or video chat with you, you will see a notification in the upper right corner of the screen. Choose to answer with video, voice, or decline the call.

Figure 5.43: Incoming Call Notification

To dial and call a telephone number (charges may apply) you can click on the phone receiver icon in the upper left corner of the main Skype window. Dial the number to place the call.

Figure 5.44: Phone Call Dial Pad

Next we will look at using the Calendar app to manage multiple schedules and to notify contacts for shared appointments and reminders.

Calendar

The Calendar App in Windows 8.1 can be used to schedule appointments, receive reminders of upcoming events, and invite contacts to meetings. You can also use it to sync with your Google Calendar by configuring options in the Settings Charm.

Open the App Commands (right-click or swipe down from top) to view the calendar schedule. You can choose to view a daily, weekly, or monthly calendar.

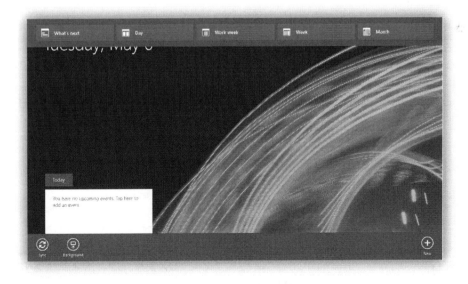

Figure 5.45: Calendar App Commands

To set a new appointment, either open the App Commands and click New, or double-click the day you wish to add an appointment to.

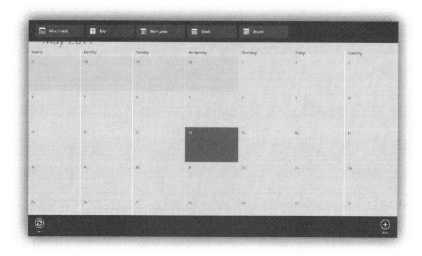

Figure 5.46: Calendar View App Commands

When you double click on a calendar day to enter a new appointment, you can enter the subject, choose the user calendar you would like to add the appointment to, and add additional details if you would like. Once the appointment has been saved you will see it listed on your schedule.

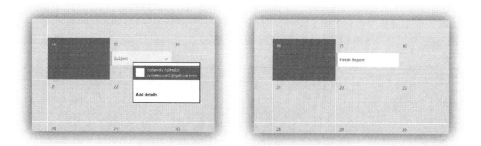

Figure 5.47: Select Calendar And Details and Appointment Added To Calendar

Once you have clicked the New button in the app commands or double-clicked on the desired date and selected Add Details, you will see the new appointment screen. In the left pane, you can set a number of options such as the date, time, length, and location. Expanding the options out gives other settings you can configure for the event, such as selecting the contacts that you would like to notify about the event. In the right pane, you can type the message title, along with a more detailed description of the message below. Click the save button in the upper-right corner to save the appointment. Click the delete button next to the save button to delete the appointment.

Figure 5.48: New Appointment Screen

After creating the appointment, you will find it listed in the main calendar window. To change your view to a day, week, or month view, open the app commands and select the appropriate button.

In Windows 8.1, Microsoft has leveraged many of the multimedia features available on the Xbox 360 and Xbox One to provide an immersive experience for Windows 8.1. In the next few sections we will explore these apps – Xbox Video, Xbox Music, and Xbox Games.

Xbox Video

The Xbox Video app is the Windows 8.1 default video player for touch screen devices. Xbox Video allows you to stream 1080p HD movies and TV shows through the service. You can also rent movies and TV shows for a one-time viewing. Content purchased through the Xbox Video service can be purchased once, and then viewed on any of your Xbox 360, Xbox One, Windows Phone 8, and Windows 8.1 & Windows RT devices. When the app first opens, scrolling to the right shows a number of recommendations and categories for purchasing content through the store. Scrolling to the far left provides you with your video library. Here you can explore your own videos for playback. Right-clicking or swiping down on a touch screen will display the app commands for the Xbox Video App. While a video is playing in the Now Playing window, tapping on the touch screen or clicking with your mouse will show playback options, such as pause, skip ahead, and rewind.

63

Figure 5.49: Xbox Video App

Videos you have stored on you system will be located to the far left of the app. You can open your files from this section, and add folders to your library so they are shown in this section as well. To open a file from another location on the PC, right-click or swipe down from the top edge to open the App Commands, then select Open File.

Figure 5.50: Open File App Command Option

From this screen you can navigate to the location of the video file you wish to open. Select the file and click the Open button.

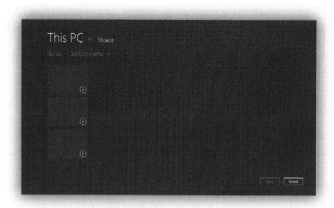

Figure 5.51: Browse For File To Open

Clicking the Search button (magnifying glass) in the upper right corner will open a search box. Enter the name of the movie or TV show you wish to find.

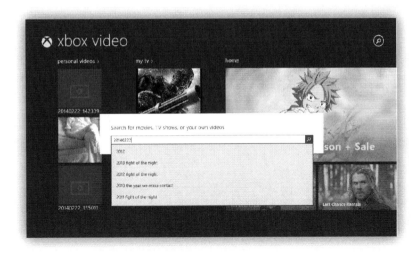

Figure 5.52: Search For Show Or Movie

You can view movies and television shows in the spotlight section by clicking on the category name. When you select a specific show or movie, you will be taken to that title's page where you can view pictures and details about the show. By clicking on a season or listed episode, you can purchase a season, a season pass for currently airing shows, or individual episodes.

Figure 5.53: Purchasing Options and Episode Synopsis for a TV Series

If you own an Xbox 360 you can use the Play to Xbox 360 option to play the movie or TV show on your Xbox 360 console. You can also use the Share charm on the Charms menu to share your favorites with friends.

While playing a video, you will see the Now Playing window (Figure 5.54), which allows you to skip forward or back, pause, and adjust other playback options.

Figure 5.54: Xbox Video Now Playing Window

Now that we have looked at the Xbox app for watching videos we will explore the Xbox app for audio.

Xbox Music

The Xbox Music app is the default music player in Windows 8.1 touch screen devices and is a hub for streaming and purchasing songs and albums. Your personal music library is located in the Collections section on the right. Songs and albums can be purchased and added to your library, or music can be streamed for free with the Xbox Music app Radio feature.

Figure 5.55: Xbox Music App Screen

Your collection can be sorted by album, artist, or song. Double-clicking an item in the collection will open the artist page. From here you can view other songs from this artist that you own and see other albums and tracks you can purchase or stream.

Figure 5.56: Xbox Music App Commands

When you begin playing an album you will see a listing of all the tracks on the album.

Figure 5.57: Track List And Playback Options

When you click a track in the list you will see a "+" icon. Click this icon to add this track to your Cloud collection of music or add this track to a playlist.

Figure 5.58: Add Track To Cloud, Playlist, Or Now Playing

App Commands in the Music App let you play the selected item, add the item to a playlist or collection, start the streaming radio service, and get more information about the track and artist.

Figure 5.59: App Commands

The "..." button under an album in the collection will allow you to start the radio service for the listed artist, pin the item to the Start Screen, delete the album, and match album information online.

Figure 5.60: Album Context Menu

Controls for playback of the current track are at the bottom of the window. You can skip back or ahead tracks, pause/play, adjust the volume, and repeat/randomize.

Figure 5.61: Playback Controls

The Radio section is used to stream music based on artists that are similar to the artist you select. To start a new station click the Start A Station button.

Figure 5.62: Streaming Radio Section

Type in one of your favorite musician's names or click on a station you have already created to begin streaming.

Figure 5.63: Search For An Artist Station

The Explore section highlights popular artists and new albums you may be interested in.

Figure 5.64: Explore Section

69

The Now Playing window shows the track list for the current selections. If you are using the Radio streaming feature, you'll see upcoming tracks in this list.

Figure5.65: Now Playing Window

With the Xbox Music app there are millions of songs that you can stream, download, and own. You can stream tracks, download your favorite tracks, create playlists, and create streaming stations based on artists you love.

Next we will look at the Xbox Games app that is used for browsing and purchasing Windows games.

Xbox Games

The Xbox Games app lets you view the Xbox Games marketplace, view Xbox Live friends and activity, and view featured Windows Games from the Windows Store. You can download and play Xbox Games for Windows 8.1 and earn game achievement points.

Figure 5.66: Xbox Games App Initial Screen

By Scrolling to the left side of the screen you will be able to sign into Xbox Live and interact with your Xbox Live friends. While the Xbox Video, Music, and Games apps provide content from Microsoft to your PC, the Photos app can pull pictures from not only your PC, but also your Facebook account, Flickr account, and OneDrive.

Photos

The Photos app can be used to access photos on your PC, as well as photos shared through various cloud storage providers. Select the location of the pictures you wish to browse, and scroll through the available images.

Figure 5.67: Photos App Start Page

Once a library is open, you can either browse all images, or select specific images by right-clicking or swiping down on the image. The selected photos can then be printed or shared via the Charms Bar.

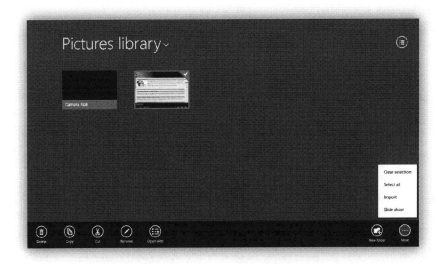

Figure 5.68: Photos App Selected Item App Commands

Opening the App Commands provides sort and selection options, as well as the option to view images as a slide show and import pictures from a camera.

Figure 5.69: Photos App Commands

Now that we have looked at the app for viewing photos on your Windows 8.1 PC, we will look at using the Camera app to take pictures and video.

Camera App

When you launch the Camera app you can click the camcorder icon to record video and the camera icon to take a photo. The timer and exposure buttons let you adjust those settings from the App Commands.

Figure 5.70: Camera App Main Window

After you have recorded a video in the app, you can play it back and trim the video selection with the Trim option in the App Commands.

Figure 5.71: Recorded Video Playback

Use the Trim button under the video playback App Commands to adjust the length of the video.

Figure 5.72: Video Playback App Commands

The App Commands for a photograph let you resize, crop, and edit the photo.

Figure 5.73: Photo App Commands

Clicking the Edit button will open the Photo Editor. This feature is used to make changes to a picture such as adjusting the lighting and color. You can Auto Fix the photo to resolve many common issues, and the Effects button will add enhancements to the image.

Figure 5.74: Photo Editor Window

With Windows 8.1, Microsoft has emphasized the benefits of their OneDrive cloud storage platform. In the next section we will go over how to use the service and upload files to the cloud.

OneDrive

OneDrive is Microsoft's cloud storage platform for storing pictures, documents, and other files in the cloud. By signing into your Microsoft Account you can access your OneDrive from any supported PC, tablet, and phone. You can also configure sharing and access to others, so that you can easily share pictures with family without sharing other personal files stored on OneDrive.

You can select folders in your OneDrive account from the main OneDrive screen. From here you can browse folder contents or you can choose to add files and modify sharing settings. Clicking the folder tile will open the specified folder in the OneDrive App.

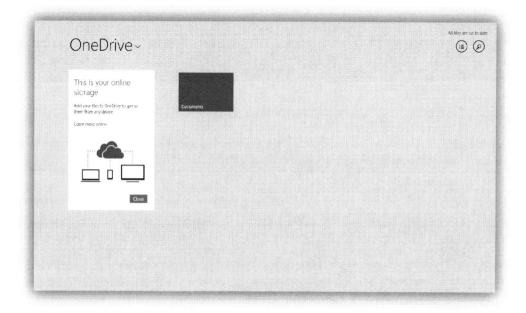

Figure 5.75: OneDrive Initial Screen

To upload a file to your OneDrive, navigate to the OneDrive folder you want to upload to. Next open the App Commands and click the Add Files button.

Figure 5.76: OneDrive Pictures App Commands

Browse for the files you wish to upload by navigating the folder structure in the upper-left portion of the screen. You can then select the files to upload and click the Copy To OneDrive button. Depending on the file size, this may take some time to upload the selected files to the cloud.

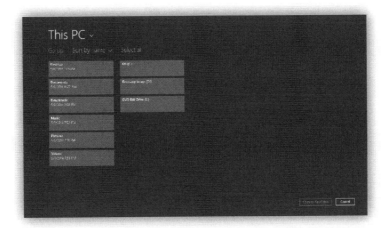

Figure 5.77: Browse Files to Upload

When the upload is complete, your file will be available through your OneDrive account on other devices, and through programs (such as Microsoft Word 2013) that support accessing OneDrive cloud storage.

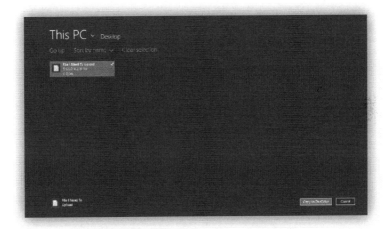

Figure 5.78: Select Files To Upload

App Commands for files and folders in your OneDrive account let you move/copy a file, create a new folder, and share access to files.

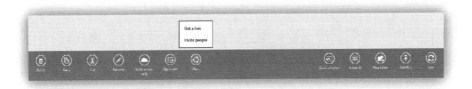

Figure 5.79: OneDrive App Commands

The New Folder icon can create new subfolders in your OneDrive account. You can then invite contacts to access the files that you have chosen to share with them.

Figure 5.80: Create A New Folder

Files and folders stored on your OneDrive account can be shared so that others can view or edit the files. To invite others to view or modify your file, select the file or folder you wish to share and select the Share option from the App Commands.

Getting a link will save a link path to the file in your clipboard. Simply paste the link in an email or message to let others access the file with the selected privileges.

Figure 5.81: Get A Link To Shared Content

You can launch the Share Charm to immediately paste the link into the Mail app or other program.

Figure 5.82: Share Charm

If you choose the Invite People option under the Share icon, you can email invitations to contacts. Enter their email address, a note, and select privileges and requirements for a Microsoft Account.

Figure 5.83: Invite People to Shared Content

The OneDrive service will automatically sync files on your PC to the Cloud and any new files in your OneDrive account will be synced to this PC. In the Desktop Taskbar you will notice the OneDrive application running in the background. To view files in your OneDrive account you can right click the icon on the Taskbar or click on OneDrive in the left pane of File Explorer.

Next we will take a look at the News App in Windows 8.1 – a great way to stay up-to-date on current events.

News

The News App in Windows 8.1 is a news hub with a graphically rich layout for news articles compiled from a number of media sources. Clicking on the news headline will expand out the full article's text. Clicking the back button will take you back to the main News app window.

Simply scroll to the right to view article headlines and video content from your selected news sources.

Figure 5.84: News App Top Stories

The News app can be customized by selecting your preferred news sources for articles and content. You can choose the type of content and media sources you receive via the News App by opening the App Commands, as seen in Figure 5.85.

Figure 5.85: News App Commands

In the app commands, select Sources to choose the news sources you would like to use with the News app.

Figure 5.86: News App Sources

By selecting the news sources that interest you, you can customize the app to quickly deliver only content you are interested in by the content providers you trust.

Bing Health and Fitness

The Bing Health and Fitness App features articles and tips to aid you in staying healthy, fit, and active. Click on any of the featured articles to read more or learn new exercises and tips. On the far right side of the app, you will find links for tracking your diet and health. You can also access quick links to exercises, workouts, nutrition, and your personal trackers, all through the App Commands.

Figure 5.87: Bing Health And Fitness Main Window and App Commands

Now that we have looked at the new Bing Health and Fitness App, we can explore the new Bing Food and Drink App to search for some healthy recipes.

Bing Food and Drink

The Bing Food and Drink App lets you browse categories of recipes and drinks, search for specific recipes, and produce a shopping list based on recipes you plan to make.

Figure 5.88: Bing Food And Drink Main Window

This app offers step-by-step recipes for a wide array of meals, desserts, and drinks. Simply scroll through the featured recipes or search results and add the item to your Recipe or Shopping list.

In the App Commands you can navigate to Recipes, Wines, Cocktails, Tips, or have quick access to your Meal Planner and Shopping List. The Shopping List makes it easy to find all of the ingredients you need to have on hand or purchase in order to make the recipes you've selected.

Figure 5.89: Bing Food And Drink App Commands

In the next section we will look at the Windows Store. The Windows Store is an app for accessing thousands of apps for Windows 8.1 and Windows RT.

Windows Store

The Windows Store is an online marketplace for finding apps for your Windows 8.1 computers. You can browse for free apps and apps for purchase. Apps range from games and entertainment, to utilities, to productivity software. Featured apps will be viewable when you first open the app. Scroll to the right to see popular apps in a variety of categories.

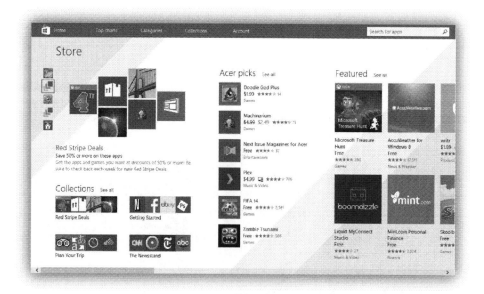

Figure 5.90: Windows Store

Along the top of the app you will notice a menu bar with links to Home, Top Charts, Categories, Collections, and Account. The Categories link will expand to show available categories of apps for download. The Account link allows you to access your account information and view apps you have previously downloaded or purchased.

Figure 5.91: Windows Store Menu

Apps purchased through the Windows Store can be installed on up to 81 devices. Updates for installed Windows Store apps are installed automatically by default. As you scroll through the main Windows Store screen, you can browse categories for different apps, as well as search for a specific title, or browse the top free games in the store. Click on a category header as you scroll to view more apps in that category, or choose and option from the Categories menu.

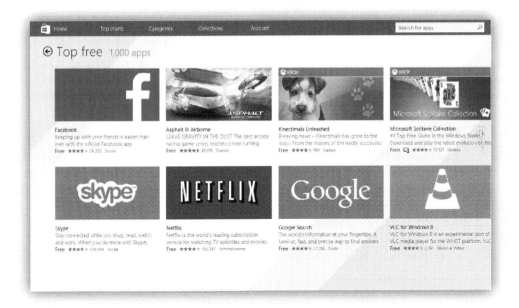

Figure5.92: Top Free Games Category

Click the app's tile to view details such as the description, ratings, reviews, pricing, and system requirements. To install the app, click the install button; otherwise you can click the back arrow in the upper-left corner of the app's description page.

Figure 5.93: Windows Store App Page

Scroll to the right on the app's detail page to view more information and ratings.

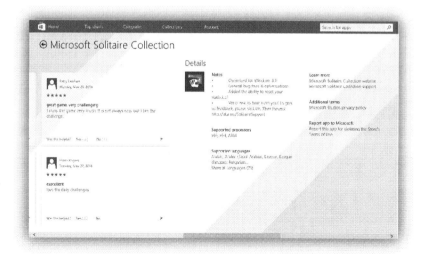

Figure 5.94: Windows Store App Page Reviews And Details

In chapter 6 we will look at Internet Explorer 11, the new Modern UI Internet Explorer 11 App, and other browsers commonly used in Windows 8.1. We will familiarize you with the layout of menus on the screen and how to perform some basic tasks as well.

Chapter Review Questions:

1. Describe what each of the four hot corners do when you click them with your mouse.
2. How do you access the App Commands on a touch screen device or on a device with a keyboard and mouse?
3. Name two ways you can close a Modern UI Windows Store App.
4. Explain what Snapping An App means and describe two ways to perform this action.

Chapter 6 - Web Browsing

Today, much of what we do on our computers relies upon accessing the internet-be it for news, e-mail, shopping, or for work. There are several popular web browsers that help us to securely accomplish these tasks.

Internet Explorer 11

Internet Explorer is currently the most widely used web browser. It is pre-installed by default in Windows 8.1. In Windows 8.1, there are two versions of Internet Explorer 11, a traditional desktop application, and a new Modern UI app that is launched from the pin on the Start Screen. Internet Explorer 11 sports a minimal user interface, leaving a large amount of screen space for the page you are viewing. There are numerous security improvements to Internet Explorer 11. Internet Explorer 11 has also added support for HTML5, the new standard for many newly designed websites.

Internet Explorer 11 Desktop Application

Figure 6.1: Internet Explorer 11 Address Bar

Internet Explorer 11 Window Layout

Internet Explorer 11 has several primary components to the program window. The title bar is the uppermost portion of the window. Located underneath the title bar and on the left side of the window, the address bar shows the web address of the current page, and is used to type in an address for a site you wish to visit. You can also use the address bar to perform a web search using the default search engine for the browser. For instance, you would type either the web address www.microsoft.com or type the word "Microsoft", and hit enter on your keyboard. This action will then search using your default search engine, using the search term "Microsoft". As you type in the Address Bar, you will see a list of websites that match the keys typed in the Address Bar, as well as favorites and sites you have visited matching the search term.

Figure 6.2: Address Bar Results

To the left of the address bar are the Back and Forward buttons. These buttons can be clicked to navigate to recently visited websites. You can right-click the button to see a list of recent sites to navigate to.

Figure 6.3: Internet Explorer 11 Forward & Back Buttons

On the upper right side of the screen you will see the Minimize, Maximize/Restore, and Close buttons that have been previously discussed. Beneath those buttons you will find three icons: The Home button, the Favorites button, and the Tools button. The Home button will take you back to your homepage, or if you right-click it, you can add or change your homepage.

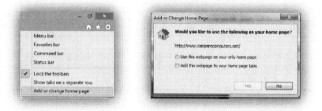

Figure 6.4: Change Home Page

The Favorites button will open your list of saved favorite websites (as well as subscribed newsfeeds and browsing history). The Favorites menu also provides a button to add the current page or current tabs to your favorites list.

Figure 6.5: Favorites Button

The Tools button has options for printing, safety options, zoom options, and various other configuration options. Safety options include deleting browsing history and InPrivate Browsing mode. You can also adjust the SmartScreen Filter settings and website checking features.

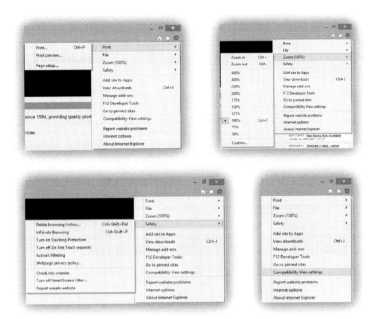

Figure 6.6: Tools Button

The Compatibility View option is located under the Tools menu. This option can be used to reload a webpage that was designed for an older web browser that may not be displaying correctly.

To configure a number of Internet Explorer settings, click on the Tools button and select Internet Options. This will open the Internet Options window. From this screen you can adjust security settings, internet connections, and manage browser add-ons and settings.

On the General Tab you can type in a homepage address, delete browsing history and related files, and adjust the appearance of Internet Explorer. The Security Tab allows you to adjust the security level for several zones. The Privacy Tab is used to manage the privacy level, control the pop-up blocker settings, and set various other privacy-related settings.

Figure 6.7: Internet Options

85

The Content Tab is used to control the Family Safety settings for web browsing, and also manages site certificates, AutoComplete settings, and RSS Feed settings. The Connections Tab is used to add manual internet connection settings. The Programs Tab can manage browser add-ons and toolbars. This tab can also configure default programs used with Internet Explorer.

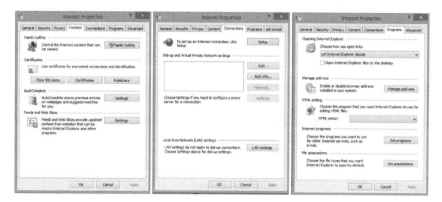

Figure 6.8: Internet Options

The Advanced Tab controls a number of settings for the browser. From here you can adjust accessibility options, browsing options, and security options for web content. I recommend leaving these settings with their default values unless a specific issue needs to be addressed.

Figure 6.9: Internet Options

Clicking the Manage Add-ons button under the Programs Tab will open a new window for adjusting Internet Explorer add-ons. Under the Toolbars and Extensions option, you can enable and disable toolbars and extensions that have been installed. Under the Search Providers option, you can adjust the order of search engines and set your desired default provider. The Accelerators options allows you to adjust the service used for the Internet Explorer Accelerators feature. Tracking Protection and Spelling Correction options let you choose lists for the provided features.

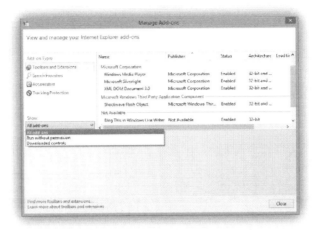

Figure 6.10: Manage Add-Ons

With Internet Explorer 11 you can have multiple tabs open. Each tab can contain a different webpage-all from within the same window. Simply click the new tab button, type the address you wish to visit, and click on the tab to switch back and forth between screens.

Figure 6.11: Open a New Tab

Opening a new tab will display commonly visited websites in the blank tab. You can either click on one of the listed sites or type in an address in the Address Bar.

If the computer is not connected to the internet, or if there is another network related issue, you may see the browser display the message "You're not connected to a network". If you see this screen, check your network connections, devices, and settings. You can also click the Fix Connection Problems button to attempt to troubleshoot the issue.

Downloading Files In Internet Explorer 11

One of the most common internet tasks is downloading a file, be it a picture, document, or installation file. Before clicking on a download link be sure the site and the content of the link are known and from a trusted source. Viruses and malware often are unknowingly downloaded by clicking on a link expecting one thing, and instead being tricked into downloading a malicious program.

 Use caution when downloading files for installing content from the web.

When you click on a download link, you will notice a small yellow bar at the bottom of the webpage prompting you to Run, Save, or Cancel. In many cases you will want to click the save button.

Figure 6.12: File Download Dialog Box

You can click the View Downloads button to view the progress of the download. By default, downloads will be saved to the Downloads folder inside of your user profile directory (ex. C:\Users\Owner\Downloads). The download will progress until complete, and will then offer the choices to Run or Open, Open Folder, or View Downloads.

If you wish to run or open the file you can do so at this time, or you can navigate to your download folder and open the file at a later time. You may want to scan any downloaded files prior to opening them if your antivirus program does not automatically scan files downloaded from the internet.

Printing In Internet Explorer 11

To print a webpage in Internet Explorer 11, click on the Options button in the upper left corner of the window. Expand the Print option and select either "Print..." or "Print Preview..."

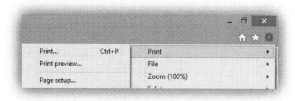

Figure 6.13: Print Menu

The Print Preview option will allow you to see a preview of how the page will be printed. You can adjust settings on this screen to modify the way the document will print.

When you click the Print button you will see the options for choosing your desired printer, along with the options for the number of copies and pages to print.

Figure 6.14: Printer Selection Window

Pin Sites to the Taskbar

To pin a website in Internet Explorer to the Taskbar simply click and drag the webpage tab down to the Taskbar and release.

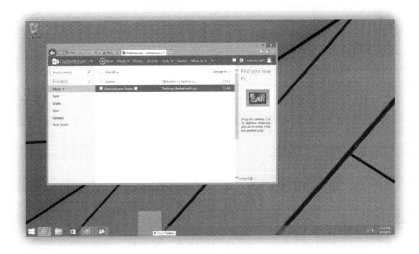

Figure 6.15: Drag Tab To Taskbar

Some web pages will have additional functionality when pinned to the Taskbar – providing Jump Lists with special features. For instance the Outlook web site will allow you to access your Inbox, OneDrive, People, Calendar, or create a new e-mail message all from the Jump List.

Figure 6.16: Pinned Web Page Jump List

To remove a pinned site you can right click the icon and select Unpin The Program From Taskbar.

Next we will look at the Modern UI Internet Explorer 11 - Internet Explorer redesigned for ease of use with a touch screen.

Internet Explorer 11 Modern UI App

The Modern UI version of Internet Explorer 11 is designed to be a full screen, touch-centric browser for Windows 8.1 touch screen devices. The address bar, navigation options, and other settings are hidden unless you open the App Commands by right-clicking or swiping from the top of the screen.

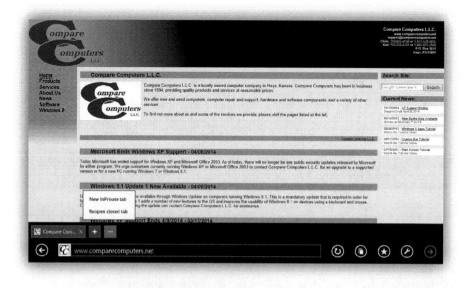

Figure 6.17: Internet Explorer 11 Address Bar

Figure 6.18: Page Tools

Swipe down from the top of the touch screen or right-click the screen to open the address bar in the Internet Explorer 11 app. When you start typing in the address bar, Internet Explorer 11 will display pinned, frequent, and favorite websites that match your entry in the address bar. You can also type a search term directly in the address bar. The Internet Explorer 11 app's back button is located next to the address bar in the lower left corner of the app command window. To the right of the address bar, you will find an icon for the refresh page button, pin site button, page tools button, and the forward button. Refresh simply reloads the current page. Pin site will pin the current webpage to your Start Screen for quick access. Page Tools provides options for Get App for This Site on supported web pages, Find on Page for searching, and View on the Desktop for loading the current page in the desktop version of Internet Explorer 11.

Figure 6.19: Address Results as you Type

When you right-click or swipe a touch screen from the top in Internet Explorer 11, you will see the tabs section on the AppBar above the Address Bar. Open tabs will be ordered along the top, and can be closed by clicking the "X" in that thumbnail image. To open a new tab, click the "+" button in the upper right corner of the AppBar. Clicking the "..." button in the upper right corner of the screen opens the Tab Tools. This option allows you to open a new InPrivate tab for private browsing, and allows you to close all open tabs except the current webpage.

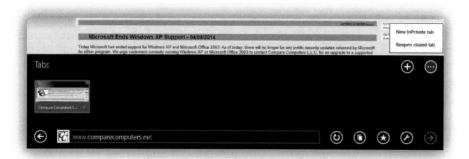

Figure 6.20: Internet Explorer 11 Tabs

Under the Options screen in the Settings Charm, you will be able to adjust the appearance of the Internet Explorer 11 app. You can change the homepage, set the Address Bar to always be shown, and adjust the Reading View font. You can also delete browsing history, passwords, and phone numbers from this screen.

Figure 6.21: Options Menu

Reading mode converts the page into a primarily text based document. You can scroll to the right while in this mode to read in a similar way that you read an article in the News App.

Figure 6.22: Reading Mode Button

This mode can make it easier to read articles and web pages that may not display correctly on all browsers.

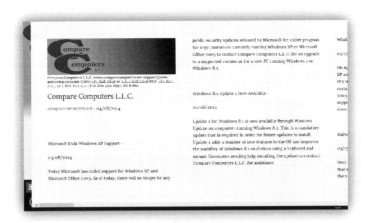

Figure 6.23: Reading Mode

Another App that can be used to read website content at a later time is the Reading List App. To save a webpage to this list open the Share Charm. Choose Reading List from the available options.

Figure 6.24: Share To Reading List App

Choose a category for the site content you are saving for later reading, then click the Add button.

Figure 6.25: Choose Category For Content

Next we will explore using the Reading List App to access our site we wish to read later on.

Reading List App

Open the Reading List App from the Start Screen. Select an item that you have added for later reading to begin viewing that content.

Figure 6.26: Reading List App And Saved Content

If multiple items are in your Reading List, click the next item in the list in the left pane. To delete a read item, right click the link in the left pane and select the trash can icon.

Figure 6.27: Viewing Content Saved In Reading List

In the next two sections we will look at Mozilla Firefox and Google Chrome-two other widely used web browsers in Windows 8.1.

Mozilla Firefox

Mozilla Firefox® is another widely used web browser designed for web standards compliance. It supports an active developer community that creates a variety of add-ons that increase the functionality of the browser.

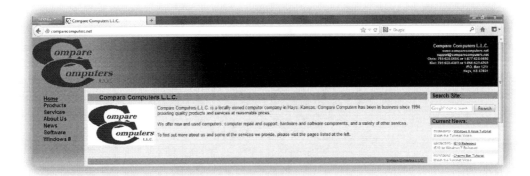

Figure 6.28: Mozilla Firefox Start Page

The Firefox button in the upper-left corner provides access to settings for displaying the web page, printing, using add-ons, and accessing bookmarks.

Figure 6.29: Firefox Menu Button

To the side of the Firefox button are tabs for the open browsing sessions. You can choose to use just a single tab, or use multiple ones by clicking the "+" tab to open a new tab.

Below those sections, you will find the back navigation button, Address Bar, and search box. Just like Internet Explorer, you can enter a web site address or a search term into the Address Bar. The search box will utilize the listed search engine for results typed into the search box. To the right of the search box you will see the home button and the bookmarks button. Clicking on the bookmarks button will expand out your bookmarks. At the top of the bookmarks menu you can find the Add to Bookmarks link. You can also click the star icon in the Address Bar to add the current page to your bookmarks.

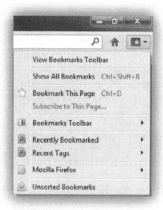

Figure 6.30: Bookmarks Menu

Figure 6.31: Bookmark Page Icon

Next we will look at how to use the Google Chrome web browser and examine some of its features.

Google Chrome

Google Chrome is another popular web browser. It features fast performance and JavaScript rendering, and excellent security. Tabs are located at the top of the window, with the navigation buttons, Address Bar/Search Bar, and settings button below the tabs.

Figure 6.32: Google Chrome

Google and the Google logo are registered trademarks of Google Inc., used with permission.

The settings button on the far right of the Address Bar can be used to print, change settings, and access bookmarks.

Figure 6.33: Settings Button

Google and the Google logo are registered trademarks of Google Inc., used with permission.

When you download a file or program in Chrome, a download progress tile will appear in the bottom left corner of your screen. When the download completes, you can click to open the item, or click on the arrow to expand out available options.

Figure 6.34: Chrome Downloads

Google and the Google logo are registered trademarks of Google Inc., used with permission.

In Chapter 7 I will explain how to access and change a number of settings in the control panel and how to connect your PC to a network.

Chapter Review Questions:

1. Describe how to access favorites/bookmarks in Internet Explorer 11, Firefox, and Google Chrome. How do you add a website to your favorites/bookmarks list?
2. Describe how to manage add-ons and extensions for each of the three browsers discussed in this book.
3. Describe the process for saving an executable file from a website to your PC.

Chapter 7 - Networking, Security, and Control Panel Settings

When you open the Control Panel link on the Start Menu, you will see a window similar to the one in Figure 7.1. The Control Panel is the primary hub for adjusting numerous system-wide settings.

Figure 7.1: Control Panel

The System and Security category provides access to security-related tasks like Windows Update and the Windows Firewall. Other system tasks can be accessed through this category as well. Here you will find system power settings and backup options.

The Network and Internet category is used to access the Network and Sharing Center and HomeGroup settings. Internet Explorer Options can also be accessed through this Control Panel category.

The Hardware and Sound category contains links to the Devices and Printers configuration as well as Sound, Display, and Power Options.

The Programs control panel category allows you to uninstall programs and manage the default programs on the PC. You can also add and manage Desktop Gadgets.

The User Accounts and Family Safety category can be used to manage user accounts on the PC and configure parental controls. Information Cards and Windows credentials can also be managed through this category.

The Appearance and Personalization section can adjust personalization and display options. Start Menu and Taskbar settings, folder options, and fonts can be adjusted through this category as well. The Ease of Access Center is used to manage accessibility options for those with disabilities. From here you can increase readability for the vision impaired, adjust settings for the hearing impaired, and set up speech recognition.

You can adjust date, time, and language settings by using the Clock, Language, and Region category in the Modern UI Control Panel.

System Information is available through the System and Security category. With the System window open you can view information about the PC and manufacturer. You can also access the Device Manager to update and manage hardware on the PC.

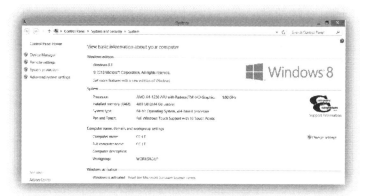

Figure 7.2: System Information

Hardware categories in the Device Manager can be expanded to expose specific hardware components on the computer. Right-clicking on an item opens a context menu, which allows you to update drivers, remove/disable the device, and view properties for the component. You can also scan for hardware changes to install drivers for unknown devices.

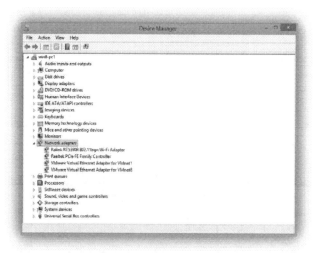

Figure 7.3: Device Manager

The Power Options settings under the System and Security category can manage the various power saving options for the PC. You can select a preconfigured plan, or manually adjust settings by clicking on the Change Plan Settings link.

Figure 7.4: Power Options

From the Edit Plan Settings window you can select power options from the drop-down list or click the Change Advanced Power Settings link to manage many other available options.

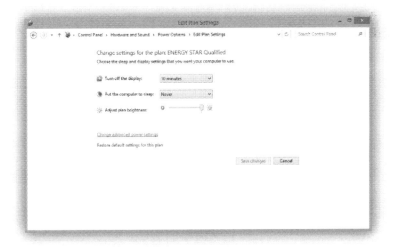

Figure 7.5: Edit Plan Settings

The Advanced Power Options Settings window provides options for sleep and hibernation, as well as settings for powering off the monitor and hard disk drive. Entering in a value of "0" will set the option to the value of "never".

Figure 7.6: Advanced Power Options

Now that we have examined the Control Panel categories, we will review managing and connecting to networks.

Connecting to a Wired Network

To connect to a wired local area network, simply connect the Ethernet cable to your PC's network interface card. Depending on your network configuration you may need to set up an IP address, or enter in a PPPOE username & password. For most home networks though, the router and PC will automatically configure your system to connect to the network and internet.

Connecting to a Wireless Network

To connect to a wireless network, be sure you have both a wireless card installed in your PC, and a wireless router or access point to connect to.

In the right corner of the Windows taskbar, and also in the Settings Charm window, you will see an icon with bars and a star. When you hover over this icon it will show that wireless network connections are available.

Figure 7.7: Wireless Connection Setup Process

Figure 7.8: Available Wireless Networks Icon In The Settings Charm

A list of available networks will appear when you click this icon. Choose your network from the list.

Figure 7.9: Available Wireless Networks

After you choose the network you want to join, click the connect button. You may see a warning about an unsecured connection if the access point is unsecured. If your access point requires a security key or passphrase to connect, type it in the window requesting the key. If you don't know what the key or passphrase is, check your router's documentation or check with your internet service provider or computer technician for assistance.

Figure 7.10: Connect to Wireless Network

⚠ Be sure your wireless router is configured to use WPA2 or higher security. Use caution when connecting to public hotspots.

If the key was entered correctly and the network configuration is correct, you will see the wireless signal bars turn white. If internet access is available, the text "Internet Access" will be listed in a small box while hovering over the network icon in the taskbar.

Figure 7.11: Internet Access

If you wish to disconnect from a specific Wi-Fi hotspot that is a saved connection you can right click the network name from the list of available wireless networks. Click the Forget This Network from the right-click context menu and saved connection settings will be deleted.

Figure 7.12

To troubleshoot network problems or access the Network and Sharing Center, right click on the network icon in the taskbar. When connecting to a public access point, keep in mind that information sent over the connection may be accessible to others without your knowledge. For your privacy and security I recommend that you limit sensitive tasks when connected to public access points. I also recommend that you use an up-to-date antivirus program and firewall.

Network and Sharing Center

The Network and Sharing Center is a central location for managing network related tasks on the PC. From this Control Panel component you can manage network and internet connections, configure network sharing options, and troubleshoot issues with the network.

To open the Network and Sharing Center, right-click on the network icon in the taskbar or select the Network and Sharing Center link from the Control Panel.

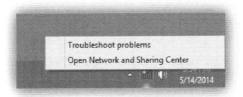

Figure 7.13: Network Context Menu

In the Network and Sharing Center main window you can view the status of your network and internet connection in the center pane. You can also set up new network connections and troubleshoot problems by clicking the links in the center pane. In the left pane you can change settings for network adapters on the PC, manage saved wireless networks, and configure sharing options. You can also open the Internet Options window, configure the Windows Firewall, and manage HomeGroup settings through links in the lower left pane.

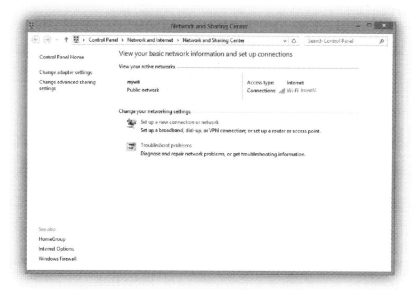

Figure 7.14: Network and Sharing Center

We will now look at managing a HomeGroup and configuring network sharing options.

HomeGroup

HomeGroup is a feature introduced in Windows 7 that allows for easy networking of home computers and devices. You can easily configure sharing access to printers, documents, and media, so that other computers can access those resources.

To set up a HomeGroup, open the desktop control panel and navigate to the Network and Sharing Center. In the lower-left corner of the window, you will find a link for HomeGroup.

Click on the HomeGroup link, and the window will open (Figure 7.15). Click the Create a HomeGroup button to create a HomeGroup.

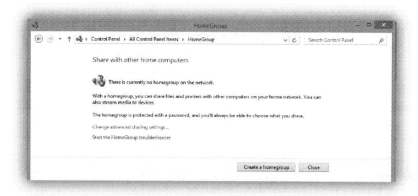

Figure 7.15: HomeGroup Control Panel Options

You will be presented with a short wizard that will walk you through the HomeGroup setup process. Click next on the first screen to begin. The next screen of the wizard lets you choose what libraries and devices you will be sharing with other computers over the network. Click the drop down box to change sharing options for each item.

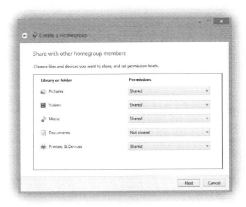

Figure 7.16: Choose Sharing Options

Use caution when enabling sharing options. Others with access to the computer or HomeGroup may be able to access or delete files that are shared.

The final screen of the wizard will provide you with a case-sensitive password that will be needed for any computer to connect to the HomeGroup. Be sure to write this password down and store it in a safe place.

Figure 7.17: Record HomeGroup Password

Sharing options for the HomeGroup can be modified at any time by opening the

HomeGroup link in the Network and Sharing Center.

Figure 7.18: HomeGroup Sharing Options

You will now be able to see content on other computers connected to your HomeGroup. Click on the HomeGroup folder on the left panel in File Explorer to access the shared HomeGroup resources. Shared printers will show as available devices when you choose to print.

In the next section we will look at setting up and managing user accounts on the PC.

User Accounts and Family Safety

In the Desktop Control Panel, the User Accounts and Family Safety section allows you to add, manage, and remove user accounts from the PC. You can also set up family safety controls to set time limits for use, allowed times for using the PC, and for setting up content restrictions for family members using the PC.

Managing User Accounts

We will need to open the desktop control panel to begin managing user accounts on the PC. On the Windows desktop, open the Settings Charm, and select the Control Panel link. Choose the User Accounts and Family Safety link in the Control Panel.

To make changes to your user account or to modify other accounts, click the User Accounts link. In the displayed window you can change the name and password for the account and also set the user as either a standard user or a system administrator.

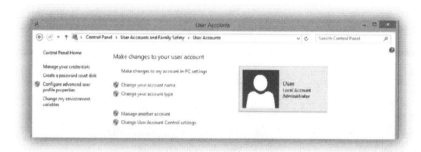

Figure 7.19: User Account Settings

To create a password for the account or to modify another account on the PC, click the Manage Another Account link. You can then choose the account you wish to change.

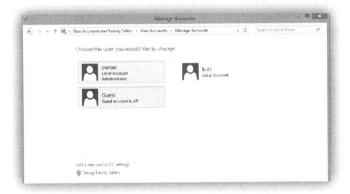

Figure 7.20: Choose User Account to Change

From here you can modify a number of settings for the selected user. Click the Create a Password link and fill in the required information to create a password for the user.

Figure 7.21: Change the Selected Account

User Accounts can also be configured using the Modern UI Control Panel options. Here you can change a local account to a Microsoft Account (note that you cannot change a Microsoft Account back into a local account); create a password, pin, or picture password; and add new users to the PC.

Figure 7.22: Add Or Manage Other User Accounts

Click the "+" icon to add a user to the PC. You will see the option to create a new local user account or a Microsoft Account in Figure 7.23. I recommend creating a local account, unless you specifically wish to use features only available with a Microsoft Account. To create a local account you can click the Sign In Without A Microsoft Account link at the bottom of the window. If you choose a Microsoft Account you will be asked to enter your Microsoft Account e-mail address and password.

Figure 7.23: Choose Your Account Type, and Select Microsoft Account Or Local Account Screens

If you choose to create a local account you will be asked to enter a username, password, and a password hint. After entering those items the account will be created.

Figure 7.24: Local User Account Prompt

Next we will look at setting up Family Safety settings for user accounts on the PC. These settings will restrict the type of content the specified user will be allowed to access and can be used to restrict the times of use.

Family Safety Management

Family safety settings can be configured by clicking the Family Safety link in the User

Accounts and Family Safety Control Panel section. To set up Family Safety, you will need a password-enabled Administrator account and a Child User account. Select the Set Up Family Safety For Any User option to begin.

Figure 7.25: Initial Family Safety Window

Click on Accounts link to create a new Child account or change an existing account into a Child account.

Figure 7.26: Edit Or Create An Account

Select the account you wish to change and click the Edit button. From the drop-down list choose the Child option. Click OK to continue.

Figure 7.27: Change Type To Child Account

Now that a Child account has been configured, you can click on the Manage Settings On The Family Safety Website link in the Family Safety Control Panel window.

Figure 7.28: Manage Settings On The Family Safety Website

This link will open your web browser to the Family Safety website where you can configure access and privileges for Child accounts on various PC's. Click on the user account you wish to restrict to view safety settings for that account.

Figure 7.29: Select The User Account To Configure

From the overview page you can see the status of each safety setting at a glance. To change a specific setting you can click on the setting name.

The Activity Reporting Summary page will list any recorded activities for the specified user. This page can be used to enable or disable activity reporting.

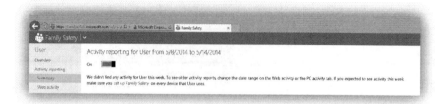

Figure 7.30: Activity Report Summary

The Web Activity Reporting page will list websites visited within the given timeframe and the action taken for the site. Use this page to enable or disable Web Activity reporting for the user account. The PC Activity Report shows days and times the PC was used during the specified date range. You can also view games, apps, downloads for the give date range.

The Web Filtering Restriction Level page is used to adjust the level of web content that is allowed for the restricted user account.

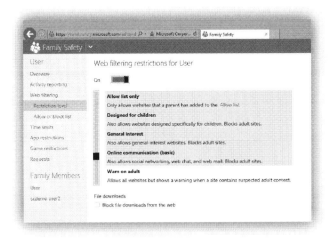

Figure 7.31: Web Filtering

The Allow Or Block List is used to grant or deny access to specific web sites. Enter the site address and click the Allow or Block button to add the site to the list.

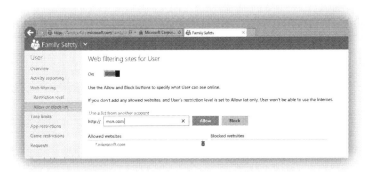

Figure 7.32: Website Allow And Block List

The Time Allowance page allows you to set an acceptable amount of time for the PC to be used per day by the restricted user.

Specific curfew hours can be set for each day of the week under the Curfew section. Click and drag your mouse cursor to highlight restricted hours on the grid.

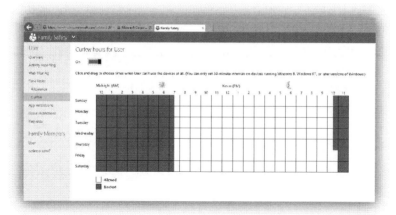

Figure 7.33: Curfew Hours

The App Restrictions section is used to allow or block specific applications from running. Scroll through the list of applications and select the apps you want to allow access to.

Figure 7.34: App Restrictions

The Rating section can limit the apps and types of games above a certain rating threshold. Adjust the slide bar to the desired rating level. Clicking the Rating System tab will show several rating providers you can choose from for rating recommendations.

Under the Game List section, you can choose to allow, deny, or rely on the game rating level for specific games already installed on the PC.

Figure 7.35: Game List

If a Child account tries to run a restricted application, they can send a request to you to grant access to the program. In the Requests From User section, you can view the pending requests and choose to allow or deny access to the program.

Figure 7.36: Request Permission

Next we will look at the User Account Control feature and how it can help protect the system from unwanted changes.

User Account Control

The User Account Control (UAC) feature helps to protect the PC by requiring administrator approval before application installation and setting changes are made that affect other users on the PC. I recommend leaving UAC at its default settings or higher, and not lowering the security level unless absolutely necessary.

> ⚠️ When you see a User Account Control alert prompting you to allow or deny a program to make changes to the computer, be sure you know the program and the action it is performing before you allow the process to continue.

User Account Control options can be accessed through the System and Security Control Panel options. Under Action Center, click the Change User Account Control Settings link. Adjust the slide bar to your desired settings, but be aware that lowering the UAC setting may put your PC at risk of malware and other security threats.

Next we will look at the built-in antivirus protection in Windows 8.1.

Windows Defender

In Windows 8.1, Microsoft has included the Windows Defender antivirus program as a built-in component to the operating system. The Windows Defender included in Windows Vista and Windows 7 was primarily an antispyware application, while the Microsoft Security Essentials was a separate antivirus program available for download. In Windows 8.1, however, Windows Defender is the Security Essentials program in all but its name. Windows Defender is a light-weight AV program that uses minimal system resources. It runs silently in the background unless an issue needs to be addressed. To open the program, you can start typing "Windows Defender" while on the Start Screen, and click on the app in the search results.

On the Home tab you can view the status of the program and start a system scan.

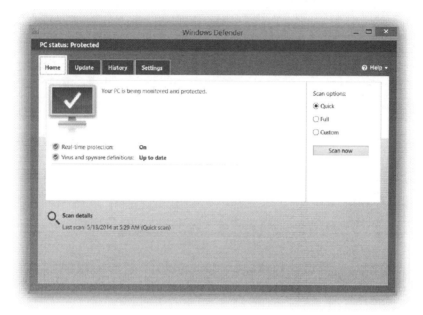

Figure 7.37: Windows Defender Main Window

On the Update tab you can manually update the AV definitions and view the status of the last update and definitions being used. The History tab offers results for previous scans. From here you can view items in the quarantine, items that were detected and allowed to remain on the PC, and a record of all previous detections. The Settings tab allows you to customize the scan settings of the program. You can disable real-time protection, exclude specific files or types from the scan, and configure advanced options. I recommend running a full scan at least once a month, along with installing any Microsoft critical security updates and patches for other programs installed on the PC.

In addition to an active, up-to-date, real-time antivirus program, another critical component is a firewall to protect against network attacks. In the next section we will explore the Windows Firewall.

Windows Firewall

The Windows Firewall in Windows 8.1 provides a two-way layer of protection for your computer by protecting against both inbound and outbound security threats. To view the firewall settings, open the System and Security Control Panel option and select the Windows Firewall link.

From the main Windows Firewall window you can configure numerous settings for the firewall. It can be enabled and disabled for certain network types. You can also customize access for specific programs and network ports.

Figure 7.38: Windows Firewall Main Window

Selecting the Turn Windows Firewall On or Off option on the left pane will allow you to turn the firewall on or off for private or for public networks. I recommend leaving both settings enabled unless you are experiencing a specific issue that requires the firewall to be disabled.

> ⚠️ Leave the Windows Firewall settings in their default configuration unless you experience a specific issue with the default settings.

Selecting the Allow an App or Feature through the Firewall link on the main window will take you to the customization page. Here you can allow specific application to pass through the firewall on public or private networks by checking the checkbox next to the application name.

Under the advanced settings for the Windows Firewall, you can create rules, allow specific port access, and many other in-depth settings. I recommend leaving this section unchanged unless you experience a specific issue that requires changing these advanced settings.

Not only is it important to use an antivirus software and firewall program, but it is also very important to keep Windows and other installed programs patched and up-to-date. Windows Update is the application that keeps Microsoft applications updated and patched for security.

Windows Update

Windows Update is used to install critical security updates and new features for Microsoft software on your PC. Your computer will check for updates and install most patches on its own with the default settings. Occasionally, some updates may require a restart of your PC to finish installing. Some updates, such as new programs not currently on your PC, may not install unless you manually select those items to install in the Windows Update program.

To open the Windows Update program, open the Control Panel and navigate to the System and Security category. Click Windows Update from the listed links to open the program. You can also access Windows Update from the Modern UI Control Panel.

In the desktop Windows Update program, press the Check for Updates link to check for the newest updates. To manually select the updates you wish to install, you can choose the link for important updates or for optional components.

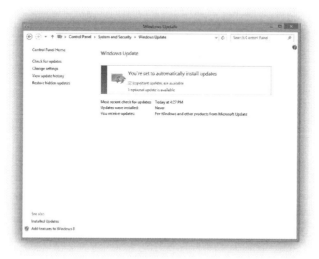

Figure 7.39: Windows Update Main Window

After clicking the link for important or optional updates, you can view both the important and optional updates by clicking on the category in the left pane. In the middle pane you will see a list of updates that are available for installation. Check items you wish to install from both sections. Click the OK button to begin when your selection is complete.

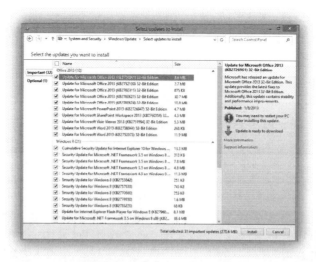

Figure 7.40: Select Updates to Install

Depending on the size and number of updates selected and the speed of your internet connection, the updates may take some time to download and install. When finished, you may be prompted to restart your computer to complete the installation.

To modify Windows Update settings you can click the Change Settings link in the left pane of the main Windows Update window. From here you can choose to automatically download or install updates and select the type of updates that will be installed.

> Allowing Windows to automatically download and install updates will help to keep your PC patched and up-to-date against security vulnerabilities.

To see a list of updates that have previously been installed, click the View Update History link in the left pane of the Windows Update window. This history of updates will list the patch name, date, type of update, and whether the update was installed successfully. If you encounter issues after installing updates, you may want to check what updates were recently installed and evaluate uninstalling them if they caused the system to become unstable.

Next we will take a look at viruses, malware, and how to protect your PC from many common threats.

Viruses, Malware, Phishing, and Securing your PC

What Are Viruses and Malware?
Viruses and malware are programs on your computer that may spread between computers, cause errors, collect information, self-replicate, change system settings, interfere with regular computer use, and/or delete or corrupt files on your computer.

How do Viruses and Malware Infect My Computer?
There are many ways that virus and malware threats can infect a computer. The list below provides several examples of ways these threats can infect your PC:

• E-mail Attachments or Embedded Code in E-mail Messages or Instant Messages.
• Visiting websites with malicious code present or malicious advertisement code.
• Downloading infected files from the web or P2P downloading programs.
• Installing free games or programs online that contain malicious code.
• Downloading or installing pirated software, music, or other files that are infected.
• Not installing Service Packs, updates, and patches for your operating system, and also for all 3rd party software currently installed on the PC.
• Not using a real-time, up to date Antivirus and Antispyware program on a regular basis.

Symptoms of a Potential Infection:
• The computer runs slower than normal or locks up frequently.

- The computer restarts on its own or crashes.
- The computer displays pop-ups, error messages, or alerts you are not familiar with.
- Your e-mail address may send out unwanted e-mails to people in your contact list.
- You receive excessive amounts of spam e-mail.
- Programs on the computer do not work normally.
- Your Antivirus is unable to download updates, run scans, or provide real-time protection.
- Security settings or firewall settings are changed on your computer.
- Shortcuts or links appear on your computer to questionable websites or programs.
- Programs, toolbars, or files you did not install may appear on the computer.
- There may not be symptoms of an infection, but threats may silently collect information.

How to protect yourself from infection:

- Install all Service Packs, Updates, and Patches for Microsoft software on the PC.
- Install all Service Packs, Updates, and Patches for all 3rd Party Software on the PC.
- Install the latest Antivirus definitions for your real-time Antivirus software and run regular full system scans.
- Install the latest Antispyware definitions for your real-time Antivirus software and run regular full system scans.
- Do not open questionable e-mails, attachments, or websites. Do not install, run, or download questionable files or programs from websites or P2P file sharing applications.
- Check the file extension before opening files or attachments, and check that the file does not contain a hidden double file extension.
- Read all security prompts carefully and do not run programs unless you are certain of their authenticity and safety.
- Scan removable storage devices to minimize the risk of re-infection.
- Use a Standard User account and password for Windows, instead of an Administrator account, to help minimize security risks and limit system wide changes.
- Use extreme caution when responding to e-mails requesting confidential information, even when the e-mails appear to be from a known sender. Phishing e-mails can be spoofed so they appear to come from a particular sender. Confirm the request for information by another means before responding directly in the e-mail. Be certain you trust websites prompting for personal or financial information, and be sure the page is secure.
- Use the Phishing Filter in Internet Explorer.
- Do not click on links in e-mails that direct you to another website, as the link's address can be spoofed. Type the address into a browser window and manually navigate to the site instead.
- Be cautious opening e-mails, even from known contacts. Just because an e-mail came from someone you know, it does not mean the e-mail, attachments, or links are safe. A Trojan may be bundled with a video or other file that someone wants to share, and they may not be aware of the hidden components of the file. Compromised e-mail accounts are commonplace, and often hijacked accounts send e-mails to all contacts using similar means to gain access to those accounts as well.
- Only install add-ons from websites that you trust. Web browser add-ons can install useful

software for your PC, but also may install malicious software. Make sure you trust the site and add-on before installing any software if prompted.

Now we will look at how to install new hardware and device drivers on the PC.

Installing New Hardware and Devices

When you first connect a new piece of hardware to your computer, Windows will need to locate and install drivers to communicate with the new device. Windows may connect to Windows Update during this process to download device drivers for the hardware. You may be prompted to insert an installation disc that came with the hardware if no drivers are found. You may also be prompted to download the drivers from the manufacturer's website. Not all hardware will be compatible with Windows 8.1, but Microsoft has worked hard to include a large number of drivers with the OS and make future drivers available online. While drivers are being downloaded and installed you may see a screen similar to the image in Figure 7.41 showing the progress of the installation.

Figure 7.41: Detecting New Hardware

Open the Control Panel and click the View Devices and Printers link to view installed hardware peripherals. The Devices and Printers section will display peripheral devices installed on the PC. Some of the items listed here are virtual hardware components, like the Microsoft XPS Document Writer and the Send To OneNote items in Figure 7.42, while others are physical hardware devices connected to the computer. You can select devices listed and view properties and settings for each device.

To set the Canon printer shown as the default printer for the PC, simply right-click on the printer and select the Set as Default Printer option.

Figure 7.42: Devices and Printers

Right-click the printer and select the Printer Properties option from the list to view properties for the printer. To print a test page, click the Print Test Page button from the Printer Properties window.

Figure 7.43: Printer Properties Window

Hardware devices can also be viewed and configured by using the Modern UI Control

Panel's Devices section.

Installed hardware devices will show up in the Device Charm depending on the app being used. If you are using the Modern UI Internet Explorer and wish to print a webpage, open the Devices charm and select the printer listed.

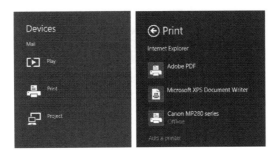

Figure 7.44: Devices Charm

You will be able to see a preview of how the printout will look and modify options (like copies, orientation, and color modes) before you print.

Figure 7.45: Print Options

Clicking the More Settings link provides even more customizable options for the printout.

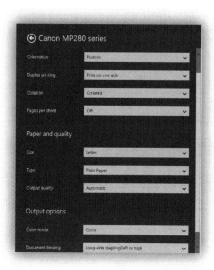

Figure 7.46: Advanced Print Options

Now that our hardware is installed, we may need to remove a piece of hardware with removable storage, like a USB flash drive or hard drive. In the next section we will look at how to safely remove the hardware from the PC.

Safely Removing Hardware

When you connect a removable storage device or other hardware, it is recommended that you use the Safely Remove Hardware feature prior to removing the device from the PC. This feature ensures the device is no longer in use and at risk of data loss and disables the device for safe removal.

When you first connect a removable device, such as a USB flash drive, you will see a brief prompt that allows you to choose AutoPlay options for that type of device.

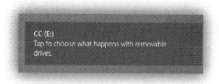

Figure 7.47: USB Flash Drive AutoPlay Option Prompt

When you click or tap this prompt you will see the available AutoPlay options for that type of media. With a USB flash drive, you can use Windows ReadyBoost to speed up the PC, set up the drive to be used as a backup drive, view files and folders, or you can take no action at all.

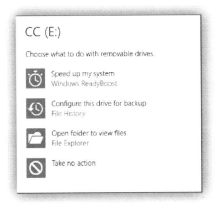

Figure 7.48: Flash Drive AutoPlay Options

When you are done working with your removable device you will need to use the Safely Remove Hardware feature. This link is sometimes hidden in the taskbar. You may need to click the small arrow icon to show hidden icons.

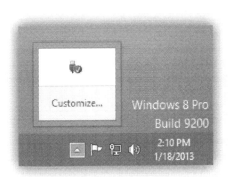 

Figure 7.49: Show Hidden Icons Arrow and Safely Remove Hardware Icon

Single left-click on the Safely Remove Hardware USB plug icon, then left-click on the device listed in the menu that you wish to remove. If Windows was able to verify the drive is no longer in use and also able to disable the drive, then you will see the message bubble that it is now safe to unplug the device. If you receive a message that the device cannot be stopped, check to make sure no programs or files are open that may be accessing the device.

Figure 7.50: Safe To Remove Hardware Balloon

125

Now that we know how to safely remove hardware we will look at how to remove installed software applications from the computer.

Uninstall Desktop Applications

Typically when a desktop application has been installed on a PC it can be uninstalled through the control panel. To uninstall a desktop program, open the control panel and click on the Uninstall a Program link. After the list of installed programs loads you can select the program you wish to remove and click the Uninstall button located at the top of the list. Follow the prompts while the program is removed. The program should be removed from the list when the uninstall is complete.

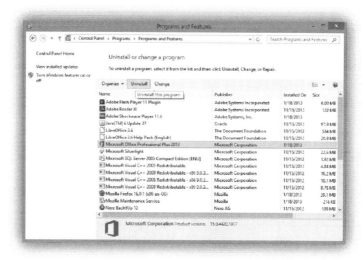

Figure 7.51: Uninstall Programs and Features

> ⚠ Use caution when uninstalling programs from the PC so that required software and utilities are not accidently removed.

In the next section we will look at using the Task Manager utility to manage actively running applications and services.

Using Task Manager

Task Manager can be used to manage programs running on the system, applications and services that load with Windows, and for viewing performance information about the PC. To open the Task Manager you can press the ALT + CTRL + DEL keys on your keyboard at the same time; right-click in the lower left corner of the screen and choose Task Manager; or you can search for "Task Manager" while on the Start Screen.

The main Task Manager window sports a very basic, streamlined interface. From this screen you can select an unresponsive program and choose the End Task option to force the application to close. Clicking the More Details button expands the window out to offer a large number of configuration options for system settings and system performance.

Under the Processes tab you can view active programs, background processes, and Windows processes; and also view the system requirements of the application in real-time. Values listed in the CPU, Memory, Disk, and Network columns are color-coded by value, so you can quickly find values that are using comparatively more resources than other active programs. Column headers will also change color if a resource is being used beyond an acceptable threshold.

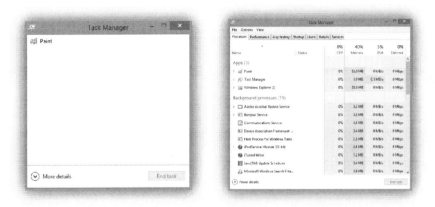

Figure 7.52: Task Manger Main Window and Processes Tab

Under the Performance tab, CPU, RAM, hard disk, and network performance is plotted in a real-time graph for use in monitoring performance to troubleshooting problems with the system. Clicking on each item will display valuable information on the hardware component, such as the CPU type and speed, and IP address. In the App History tab you can see the CPU and network usage history for various Modern UI apps on the system.

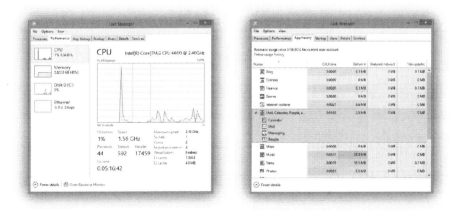

Figure 7.53: Task Manager Performance Tab and App History Tab

The Startup tab can be used to enable and disable startup applications on the computer. You can view the program, publisher, startup status, and impact on boot-up performance. Resource usage on the system can be broken down by each user account under the Users tab.

Figure 7.54: Task Manager Startup Tab and Users Tab

The Details tab contains advanced options for configuring processing on the system. This tab can control the CPU affinity, the process priority, and UAC virtualization options. These settings are for advanced users, and I recommend leaving them set to the default settings unless you know exactly what you are doing. Under the Services tab you can quickly view services and their status, as well as start and stop individual processes.

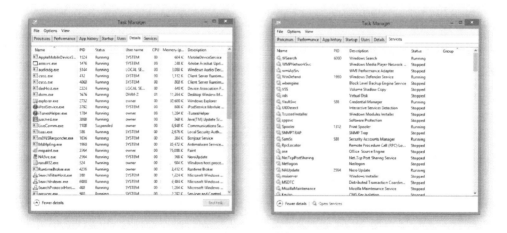

Figure 7.55: Task Manager Details Tab and Services Tab

As you can see, the new Task Manager features many improvements and new capabilities for Windows 8.1. In the next few sections I will go over the process of personalizing your PC by adjusting the themes, configuring the display options, and managing user settings.

Desktop Personalization Options

To set the display options like screen resolution, multiple monitor configuration, and refresh rate, right-click on a blank area of the desktop and select Screen Resolution from the menu.

From the screen resolution screen you can add multiple displays, change the resolution via the dropdown menu, and change the screen orientation. Clicking the advance settings link gives other options like the refresh rate for the monitor.

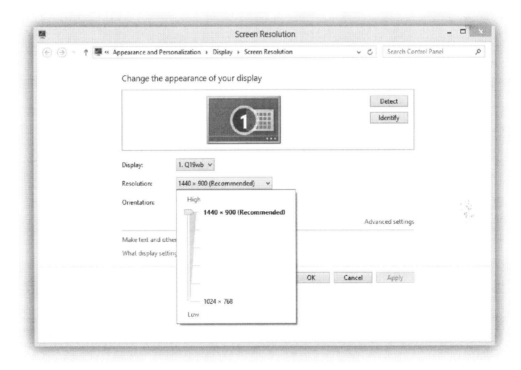

Figure 7.56: Screen Resolution Configuration

The Make Text and Other Items Larger or Smaller link will enable you to set the size of all items, or just that of the text for specific items.

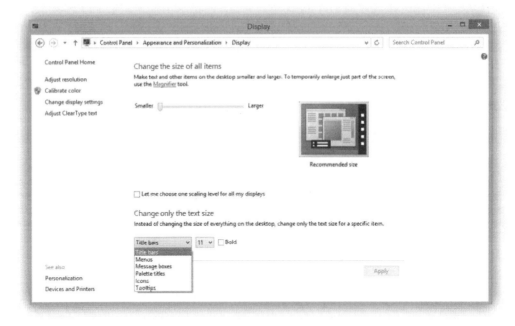

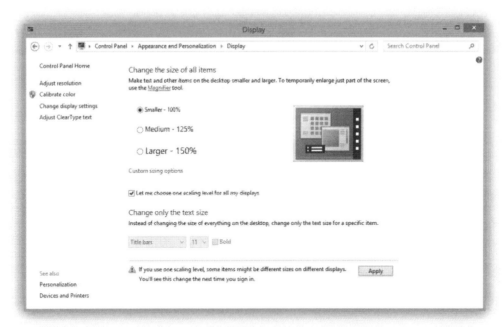

Figure 7.57: Change Size of Items and Text

To change the desktop wallpaper, theme, sound effects, and screen saver, simply right-click on a blank area of the desktop and choose the option Personalize from the list. You can choose a preconfigured theme from the list or click on one of the links at the bottom of the window to change just the wallpaper, color, sounds, or screen saver.

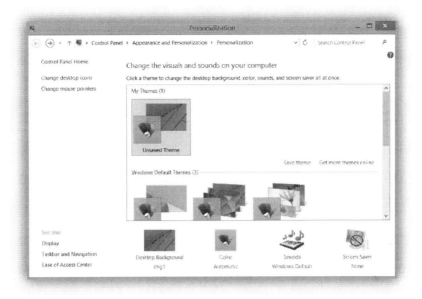

Figure 7.58: Personalization Menu

The desktop wallpaper screen lets you choose a type of wallpaper from the dropdown list. Multiple backgrounds can be selected and cycled at a specified time interval. You can also choose the fill options for the picture to fit your screen.

Figure 7.59: Set Desktop Background

Tip: To select multiple wallpapers that change after a given interval, hold the CTRL key while left-clicking wallpapers in the list or click the checkbox for each background you wish to use. Choose the desired time interval from the list and click Save Settings.

131

To change the color of the taskbar, title bars, and other controls, choose the Color option at the bottom of the main Personalization screen. From this window you can choose the color you prefer.

Many traditional settings can be configured in the desktop Control Panel, but many settings for new features in Windows 8.1 are accessible only through the Modern UI Control Panel.

Modern UI Control Panel and Personalization Options

The Modern UI Control Panel is a variant of the desktop control panel, but with a touch-based design focused on the core configuration settings. To get to the Modern UI Control Panel, open the Settings Charm and click the Change PC Settings link at the bottom of the window. You can also click the PC Settings tile on the Start Screen.

When you first open the PC Settings app, you will notice categories listed on the left and personalization options on the right. The Lock Screen, user account picture, and picture password can be configured from the links in this section.

Figure 7.60: PC Settings Main Window

When you click the PC And Devices link on the left pane, you will see new subcategories listed in the left pane. The lock screen background, background apps, and timers can be configured in this section.

The Display option is used to configure the screen resolution, adjust the screen orientation, and change the size of text and other items on the screen.

You can search for and connect to Bluetooth devices under the Bluetooth category. The Devices section manages printers and other hardware peripherals on the PC. From here you can add devices and manage settings for hardware connected to the computer.

Figure 7.61: Manage Hardware Devices

Options for your pointing device can be set in the Mouse and Touchpad section. The Typing section controls settings for spelling checks and for the touch screen keyboard. You can use the Corners and Edges section to enable and disable the App Commands, Charms Bar, and recent apps.

Figure 7.62: Corners And Edges Settings

Screen and sleep options are available in the Power And Sleep section. These options tell the PC when to take a particular action when it has been idle for a set period of time. The AutoPlay section is used to adjust the AutoPlay settings for media connected to the PC. You can view how much free space is available on the hard drive and how much is taken up by Modern UI apps in the Disk Space section. PC Info displays information about your CPU, RAM, Operating System, and manufacturer.

The Your Account section under Accounts is used to configure your identity by adding an account picture. Add a password, picture password, or PIN number to the account in the Sign-in Options section. Other Accounts is used to add and manage other user accounts on the PC.

Figure 7.63: Your Account Settings

The OneDrive category will deal with settings for the OneDrive cloud storage service. The File Storage option shows the free space in your OneDrive account and can enable saving documents to OneDrive by default. The Camera Roll section controls the quality of uploaded photos and can enable automatic photo uploads to OneDrive. The Sync Settings section will control the settings, themes, and apps that are synced when you log into a PC with OneDrive. To manage sync settings while roaming or on a capped data plan, use the Metered Connections section to adjust sync settings on these networks.

The Search setting in the Search And Apps category is used to manage personalized search results and control SafeSearch filter levels. Search history can be deleted by clicking the Clear button. The Share settings are used to adjust the apps and order of the apps that appear in the Share Charm.

Notification options can be configured on the Notification section. In this section you can adjust the apps that are allowed to notify you and how they notify you. You can also set quiet hours, during which you will not receive notifications.

The App Sizes screen displays the available space on your hard drive and the space that each app is using. Default apps can be set via the Defaults screen. On a device with a touch screen, these defaults are set to Modern UI Apps, while on a PC with a keyboard and mouse they are set to desktop applications.

The Network category contains various connection and sharing options for your PC. Under the Connection section you will find current network connections and the option to create a Virtual Private Network (VPN). Airplane Mode can be used to turn off all wireless communication. You can also disable only the Wi-Fi or Bluetooth signals. Proxy server settings can be added in the Proxy section of the Network category.

The HomeGroup section allows you to choose the types of content that you share with members of your HomeGroup. You can view your HomeGroup password to share with others so that they can connect. To disconnect from the HomeGroup and stop sharing files, click the Leave button. The Workplace section allows you to enter your user ID get workplace access and connect to internal websites and apps.

Control access to user data and devices by adjusting settings in the Privacy category. The General sections lets you allow apps to access some of your user account information and provide text suggestions based on what you type.

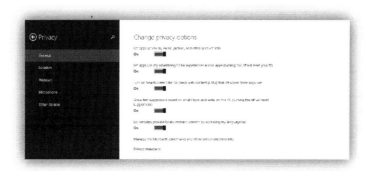

Figure 7.64: General Privacy Settings

The Location, Webcam, Microphone, and Other Devices sections control the apps that are allowed to access your computer's devices and sensors.

The Date and Time category is used to set the date, time, and time zone for the PC. Select your country from the dropdown list and select you language in the Region and Language section.

You can set up accessibility options on the PC for the vision or hearing impaired in the Ease of Access categories. The Narrator section lets you enable the text to speech narrator, configure when it loads, and adjust the voice options for the program. The Magnifier section can enable screen magnification and set tracking of the mouse or keyboard focus for magnification. High contrast themes can aide those with poor visibility. Select the desired theme from the dropdown list in the High Contrast section. The Keyboard section is used to enable the on-screen keyboard, Sticky Keys, Toggle Keys, and Filter Keys. You can adjust the cursor size and color, and to enable the keypad to control mouse movement in the Mouse section. The Other Options section contains various settings to assist those with difficulty seeing.

Windows Update in the Update and Recovery category is used to install updates on the PC. Check for new security updates and explore optional updates you may wish to install. Automatically backup versions of your files with the File History tool. To enable this feature connect an external backup device and turn the feature on. Configure your settings and begin a backup.

The Recovery section lets you refresh your PC while keeping your files or restore the PC back to original factory conditions, which will delete all of you files from the computer.

Advanced startup options can be accessed by clicking the Restart Now button under Advanced Startup. This will allow you to boot from other devices and troubleshoot problems with the computer.

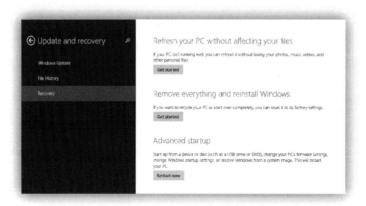

Figure 7.65: Recovery Settings

Now that we have looked at how to configure a number of settings and personalization options on the computer, we will take a look at how to perform a number of everyday tasks in Chapter 8.

Chapter Review Questions:

1. Which Control Panel category can be used to manage users and configure parental controls?
2. Describe the steps for connecting to a wireless router with WPA2 security.
3. Why do you need to be cautious of shared files and permissions on a HomeGroup?
4. What are three programs discussed in this chapter that limit the risk of virus and malware infections?
5. Describe the process for setting the wallpaper to randomly change backgrounds every 5 minutes.

Chapter 8 - Common Computer Tasks

Importing Photos From A Digital Camera Memory Card

The process of importing pictures from a memory card has changed somewhat in Windows 8.1 from previous versions of Windows. When you first connect your camera's memory card to your PC's card reader, or when you plug in your camera's USB connection to the PC, you will likely see the AutoPlay options for memory cards when the card is first connected. Tap or click on the blue notification to choose the future default action for what happens when a memory card is connected. If you choose the Import Photos and Videos option you will be able to import selected photos to your PC quickly and easily.

Figure 8.1: Memory Card AutoPlay Options

In the Photos app you can select the pictures on the memory card to import and choose the name of the destination folder. Click the import button at the bottom of the screen once the desired pictures have been selected.

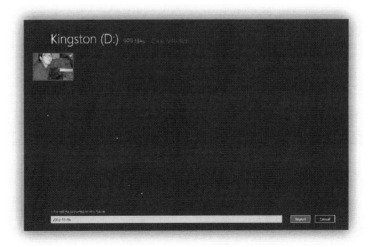

Figure 8.2: Select Pictures to Import

137

You will see a progress bar on the screen as the selected pictures are being imported. When the import is complete you can select the Open Folder button to view the imported files on your hard drive.

Figure 8.3: Import Pictures Progress

Now that we have learned how to add digital pictures to the PC we will move on to converting physical pictures into digital pictures and importing them to the computer.

Scanning a Document or Picture to a File
You may need to convert a physical photo or document into a digital file on your PC. To do this you can use a scanner or all-in-one printer. Insert the document face down on the scanner bed. The document needs to be in the corner of the scanner bed where there will usually be an arrow or mark.

Next we will use the WIA scanning feature to scan the document. Not all scanners support this feature. If you scanner doesn't have this feature, consult your scanner's documentation on how to scan using the manufacturer's software instead.

Click on the Devices and Printers link on the right side of the Start Menu. Right-click on the printer or scanner from the list that has your document or photo on its bed. Select the Start Scan option from the context menu as seen in Figure 8.4.

Figure 8.4: Context Menu Scan Option

From the New Scan window you can preview the scan and adjust the settings for the scanned image. If you are scanning a document instead of a photo, you can select a different profile from the Profile drop-down box. When you are ready to scan in the image to a file, click the Scan button. This process will take a short time, during which you will see a progress bar on the screen.

Figure 8.5: Scan Progress

After the scan is complete you will be prompted to optionally tag pictures that were scanned. Click the Import button to import the image into your Pictures library.

Figure 8.6: Import and Tag Images

Next we will work with various type of optical media and external storage, and learn how to make backups of our important pictures, documents, and files.

Optical Media and Data Backups

Working with audio CD's, DVD/Blue-Ray movies, CD-R's, DVD+/-R's, and flash drives are a common task. You can watch DVD movies using the DVD-ROM or Blue-ray drive in your PC, rip an audio CD to transfer to an mp3 player, and create backups using CD's, DVD's, and flash drives. In the following sections we will walk through the process of performing these steps.

Rip Audio From an Audio CD With Windows Media Player

To rip audio tracks from an audio CD into individual audio files on your hard drive, insert the disc in your drive and wait for the AutoPlay prompt (if it opens, select Take no Action), and search for Windows Media Player on the Start Screen and open the program.

Figure 8.7: Audio CD AutoPlay Prompt

In Windows Media Player, select the audio CD in the left pane and click the Start Rip button. You can see the progress of the rip for each individual track. By default the tracks are ripped as the ".wma" format, but you can change this setting in the Windows Media Player options section. When the rip is complete you can transfer the audio tracks to your mp3 player or listen to them through the library on your PC.

Figure 8.8: Windows Media Player Rip Progress

Burning an Audio CD With Windows Media Player

To burn an audio CD of music tracks stored on your hard drive, open Windows Media Player and click on the Burn tab in the upper-right corner. Drag files you wish to add to the CD into the burn list (right pane).

Figure 8.9: Windows Media Player Burn Tab

When you are ready to burn the disc, click the Start Burn button and wait for the process to finish. You can then eject the disc and listen to it on a CD player.

Figure 8.10: Start Burn Process

Burning Data to CD-R

When you insert a blank CD-R in your drive you will see the blue notification box the first time a blank disc is inserted. Tap or click this notification to view the blank CD AutoPlay options. We will use the File Explorer option to burn data files to the blank CD. Select that option to continue.

Figure 8.11: Blank CD AutoPlay Options

You may find an option like the one in Figure 8.12 regarding the format of the disc. In most cases I recommend that you choose the option With a CD/DVD Player instead of the Like a USB Flash Drive option. Choose the option you prefer to continue.

Figure 8.12: CD-R File System Formatting Options

A File Explorer window will open showing the contents of the blank CD. From here you can drag and drop files you wish to backup to CD.

Figure 8.13: Files To Be Burned to CD

Files you wish to add to the CD can be selected and dragged to the CD-R window. You can also select the items and from the right-click context menu, select Send To, then choose the DVD RW Drive option. Files shown in the File Explorer window for the drive are pending to be burned and are not yet on the disc. Click the Finish Burning option under the Manage tab when you are ready to burn the disc. This will open the disc burning wizard to write the data to the CD.

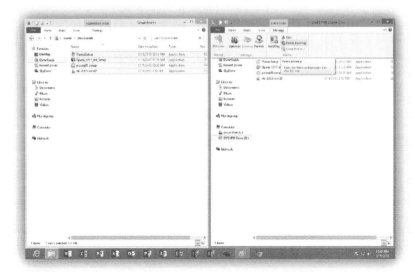

Figure 8.14: Finish Burning Option

Enter a name for the disc in the wizard and optionally select a burning speed. I recommend leaving the burning speed set at the default speed, unless you encounter an issue burning at that speed or if your media requires a different setting. Click the next button to start the burning process.

Figure 8.15: Burn to Disc Wizard

Burning Data to a DVD+R

When you insert a blank DVD in your drive you will see the blue notification box the first time a blank disc is inserted. Tap or click this notification to view the blank DVD AutoPlay options. Use the File Explorer option to burn data files to the blank DVD. Select that option to continue.

144

Figure 8.16: Blank DVD AutoPlay Options

A File Explorer window will open showing the contents of the blank DVD. From here you can drag and drop files you wish to backup to DVD. When you are ready to finalize the disc and burn the data to the DVD, click the Finalize Disc option under the Manage tab. You can then name the DVD and finish the burning wizard.

Figure 8.17: Files To Be Burned to DVD

DVD Playback in Windows 8.1

In order to play back DVD movies in Windows 8.1, you will need to install a desktop program or a Windows Store app with DVD playback capabilities. Windows 8.1 no longer has built-in support for DVD playback without the use of a third-party program. VLC media player is a free media player that can be used for DVD playback in place of Windows Media Player. Once installed, VLC Player will be available via the AutoPlay options when a DVD movie is inserted in the PC.

Figure 8.18: DVD Movie AutoPlay Options

Choosing the option to playback the DVD with VLC player will open the VLC player main window. Playback options are located at the bottom of the window. There are a variety of desktop applications and Windows Store app with similar capabilities.

Figure 8.19: VLC Media Player Main Window

Next we will look at backing up our data to external storage devices.

Backing Up Data to an External Drive

To back up files to an external hard drive you can either drag-and-drop files to the drive in the same way that you did with a burnable CD or DVD, or you can use the Windows File History tool to save backup copies of your files to an external drive.

> **Tip** Be sure to back up your data to an external storage device to minimize the risk of data loss. Verify data on the backup is valid and up-to-date.

When you first connect an external storage device you will see a window prompting you to choose the default action when a removable device is connected. If you plan to always use removable drives for File History backups you can select that option from the list. Otherwise, you can choose the Take No Action option.

Figure 8.20: Removable Storage AutoPlay Options

To open the File History tool if you did not choose the File History AutoPlay option, open the Control Panel. Select the System and Security link and then File History. Click the Turn On button if File History is not already enabled.

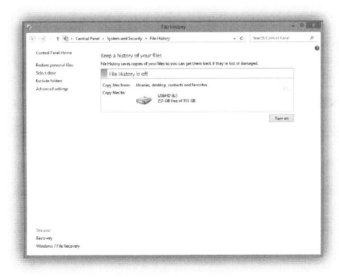

Figure 8.21: File History

To choose advanced options for backups you can select the Advanced Options link in the left pane. From this screen you can configure how often to backup files, the amount of offline storage cache, and how long to keep saved versions. You can also allow HomeGroup access to the drive if you want to enable the feature.

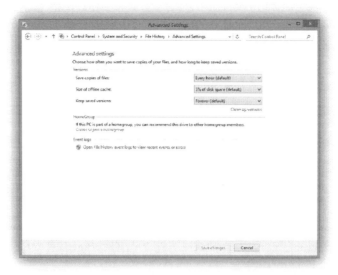

Figure 8.22: File History Advanced Settings

If you choose to manually copy files to the external storage you will notice a file copy progress window showing the progress of the transfer, the source and destination, and options to pause or cancel the transfer.

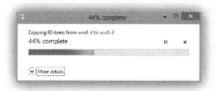

Figure 8.23: File Copy Progress Window

Clicking the More Details link expands the window to show a graph with the transfer speed and file details.

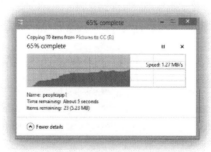

Figure 8.24: Detailed File Copy Progress Window

If the destination already contains a file with the same filename, you will see a window asking if you would like to replace the file in the destination folder with the file from the source folder.

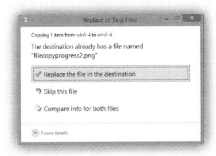

Figure 8.25: Replace or Skip Files Prompt

You can also choose the Compare Info for Both Files option to view details about both files before choosing which to replace. This window will display the name, modification date, and file size of both copies, and allows you to quickly choose options for multiple files as well.

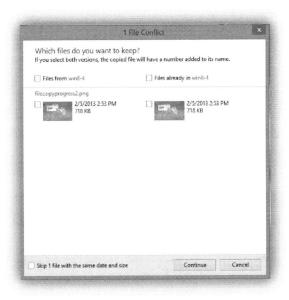

Figure 8.26: Choose Files to Keep

Next we will look at changing the default program used to open a file on your PC.

Selecting the Default Program for Opening a File

Sometimes when you double-click a file to open it will open with a program you didn't want to use. To change the default program used for opening that type of file, open the Control Panel. Under the Programs link, select Default Programs. Choosing the Set Default Programs link will open a window that lets you set specific programs as the default and manually choose defaults for the program.

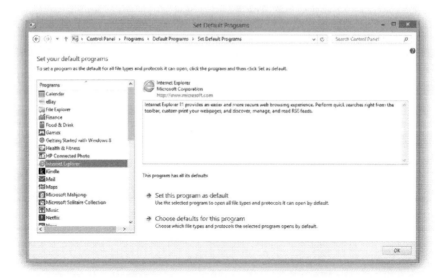

Figure 8.27: Set Default Programs Window

The Choose Defaults For This Program link can be used to associate a file extension that will be opened with the specified program. Check any extensions you would like to have opened with that program by default, then click Save.

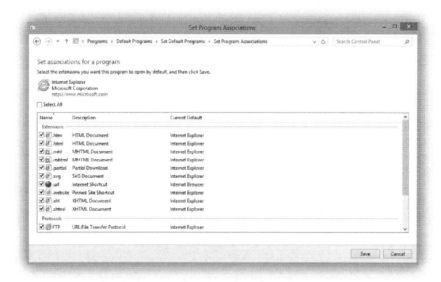

Figure 8.28: Set Program Associations Window

Back in the Default Programs Control Panel window, click on the Associate A File Type Or Protocol With A Program link. This windows will list all file types and protocols on the PC. Select the extension you wish to open with a different default program, then click the Change Program button.

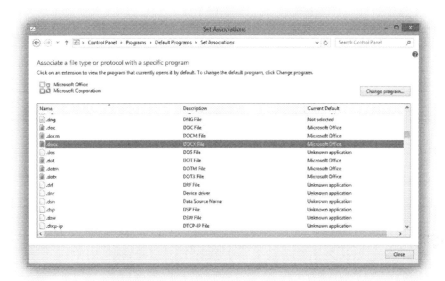

Figure 8.29: Set Associations

Scroll through the programs listed and click the app you wish to use. If the app is not listed, click the Look For Another App On This PC link to browse for the executable file you want to use to open the extension.

Figure 8.30: Change Default Program

You can also right-click a file you want to open and select the desired program from the Open With list. If the program is not listed, click the Choose Default Program link and select the desired app.

Figure 8.31: Open With… Choose Default Program

In the next section, we will look at several commonly used programs that are compatible with Windows 8.1.

Chapter Review Questions:

1. Using a Live File System when burning a CD-R limits compatibility with versions of Windows older than what release?
2. How do you manually limit the number of Windows Backups kept on an external storage device?
3. Copying your documents to a Backup folder on your C: drive is a good method for backing up files – True or False. Why?
4. Name three programs that can be used to play DVD movies in Windows 8.1.

Chapter 9 - Commonly Used Programs

Apple iTunes

Apple iTunes is a widely used program to manage music, movies, and other content on your PC. The program is also used to purchase content through the iTunes Store. You can use iTunes to transfer music and movies from your PC to your iPod, iPhone, and iPad.

Playback controls are located in the upper left corner of the window, your libraries are available via the dropdown menu on the left side, your playlists are located in the center, and the iTunes Store link is located on the right.

Figure 9.1: Apple iTunes Main Program Window

Figure 9.2: iTunes Application

You can purchase individual songs, albums, movies, and TV shows in the iTunes Store. Click the dropdown next to each category to select a genre to browse.

Figure 9.3: iTunes Store

To play music or movies from your library, choose the desired library from the left dropdown menu and select the tracks you wish to listen to. From here you can create playlists and select tracks to sync to your mp3 player.

Figure 9.4: iTunes Music Library

Windows Essentials

The Windows Essentials software package includes many feature-rich programs including an e-mail client, a photo editor, and a blog authoring tool. To download the package visit: "download.live.com". Run the installer and select the programs in the package you wish to install.

If you are unable to install Windows Essentials due to the .Net Framework 3.5 or earlier not being enabled on the PC, open the Control Panel and navigate to the Programs group. Click on the Turn Windows Features On Or Off link. Select the .NET Framework 3.5 option in the list so that a box or checkbox appear. Click the OK button to finish adding the feature to the PC. You may need to restart the PC before attempting to install the Windows Essentials suite again now that the prerequisites have been installed.

Windows Live Mail

Windows Live Mail is one of the most commonly used free e-mail clients in Windows 8.1. Previous version of Windows included a built-in e-mail client, but in Windows 8.1 the e-mail client is part of the free Windows Essentials program and is not part of a clean Windows 8.1 installation. Some manufacturer's may include the Windows Essentials package with their new PC's, however. To download Windows Essentials, visit download.live.com.

Windows Live Mail has a layout somewhat similar to its predecessors. The Ribbon UI along the top of the screen will contain common tasks under each tab heading. The left-pane contains storage folders for accounts configured in the program, as well as links to the Mail, Calendar, Contacts, Newsfeeds, and Newsgroups portions of the program. The middle-pane lists e-mail messages that are in the selected e-mail account folder. To the right of the e-mail list, you will see the e-mail Preview Pane. This section will display a preview of the selected e-mail message. The far right-pane will display a calendar and appointment reminders.

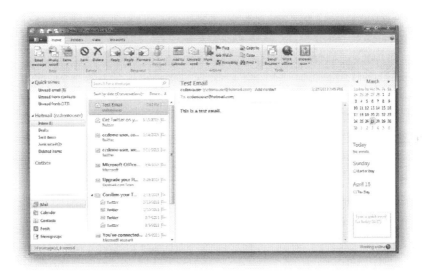

Figure 9.5: Windows Live Mail

To set up your e-mail account in Windows Live Mail, click on the blue menu button in the upper-left corner. Choose Options from the drop-down list and select E-mail Accounts. Click the Add button in the Accounts window to configure settings for accessing the e-mail account.

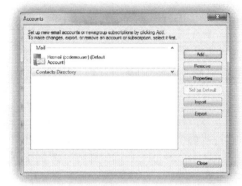

Figure 9.6: E-mail Accounts Options

Select E-mail Account from the Account Type box followed by the Next button.

Figure 9.7: Add an Account

In the Add Your E-mail Accounts window, enter the e-mail address, password, display name, and manual mail server settings if needed. If you are unsure of your e-mail server settings, contact your e-mail service provider to obtain the correct settings for your service. Enter the settings in the manual server configuration window, and click the Next button to finish the wizard. After completing the wizard, Windows Live Mail will attempt to download e-mails for the account. If you receive any errors, verify your account and mail server settings are correct.

Figure 9.8: Add E-mail Account and Manually Configure Server Settings

The Home tab contains many of the common elements used for most tasks. The E-mail Message link is used to create a new, blank e-mail message. Photo E-mail will create a new e-mail message with attached pictures. The Items link can be used to create new calendars, tasks, and other items. To delete a selected message or mark the message as junk, simply click the Delete or Junk buttons on the Home tab. To respond to a selected e-mail, click the Reply, Reply All, or Forward buttons on the Home tab. Items in the Actions group on the Home tab can be used to mark or flag messages, and to locate or copy text. The Send/Receive button is used to check for any new e-mails and send any pending e-mails. The button on the right side of the Home tab is the Windows Live sign-in button. Certain features in Windows Live Mail may prompt you to sign in with your Windows Live account or Microsoft Account. These credentials may be different than your e-mail address and password used in Windows Live Mail. If you don't have a Windows Live account or Microsoft Account, you can create one for free online.

Figure 9.9: Home Tab

The Folders tab contains options for creating new storage folders, as well as managing and navigating messages in folders.

Figure 9.10: Folders Tab

The View tab contains options for managing the views and layout of the program. Grouped conversation mode can be turned on or off from this tab as well.

Figure 9.11: View Tab

The Accounts tab can create new e-mail and newsgroup accounts and display the properties for existing accounts.

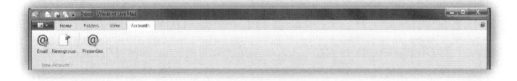

Figure 9.12: Accounts Tab

To create a new e-mail message, click the E-mail Message link on the Home tab. A new window will open with a blank e-mail message.

Figure 9.13: Email Message Button

If you have saved contacts in your Contacts list, they will appear in a list as you type their name or e-mail address in the "To…" field. You can also click the "To…" button to select contacts from your Contacts list. Enter an e-mail subject in the Subject field and your e-mail text in the area below the Subject line. You can adjust the font options in the e-mail text through settings in the Message tab. To attach a file, such as a document, picture, or other file, click the Attach File link. To check spelling in your e-mail message, click the Check Spelling button on the right side of the Message tab.

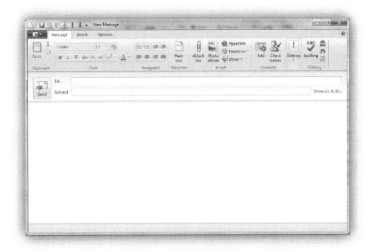

Figure 9.14: New Message Window

Clicking the Photo Album button allows you to add multiple pictures into a photo album. This feature requires a Windows Live account. Enter your Windows Live or Microsoft Account login information, or create an account for free if you do not already have one.

On the Insert tab, you can include a file attachment (document, picture, PDF), business card, or signature. You can also insert a divider line in the document text. Photos can be added as a regular attachment, or as a single photo or photo album. As a reminder, some photo features require a free Windows Live or Microsoft Account. Hyperlinks and emoticons can be added to the document text through the Insert tab as well.

Figure 9.15: New Message Insert Tab

The Options tab provides methods for encrypting, signing, and encoding your message, as well as the option to send the e-mail later. Encrypting the e-mail will help to ensure the contents of the message are more secure against eavesdropping.

Figure 9.16: New Message Options Tab

When you receive an attachment in an e-mail, you will see the file's icon at the top of the message window (Figure 9.17). Right click the attached file for options to open or save the attachment. Clicking the Open option will open the file with the default program. If no installed program can open that file type, you may be prompted to locate a program that can open the file. The Save As option will allow you to save the selected file with a specified name and location. The Save All option can be used to save all attached files in the current e-mail message to a location on your computer.

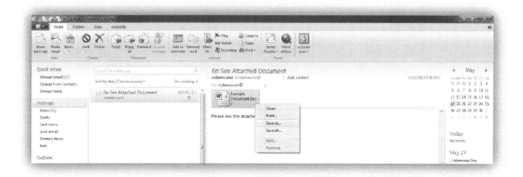

Figure 9.17: Saving Attachments

Now that we have explored setting up and accessing your e-mail, and sending new e-mail messages, we will look at the calendar portion of Windows Live Mail.

To access the calendar in Windows Live Mail, click on the Calendar link in the lower-left corner of the main program window. In the left pane you will see a small calendar and options for the types of calendar displayed. In the middle pane you will see the daily, weekly, or monthly view. To create a new event on the calendar, click the Event button on the Home tab.

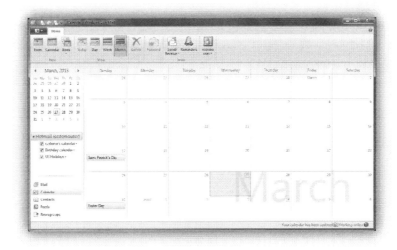

Figure 9.18: Calendar

In the New Event window you can create a subject name and location for the event. The date and time can be set by selecting from the drop-down menus on the screen. From the Event tab, you can save the event and forward it to recipients. You can also set reminders and choose the calendar name to save the event to.

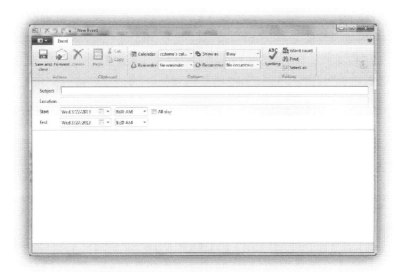

Figure 9.19: New Event Window

Clicking on the Contacts link in the lower-left corner will take you to the Contacts List in Windows Live Mail. The Home tab in the Contacts List can be used to add contacts and create categories for contacts. You can edit contact information by selecting the contact from the list and clicking the Edit Contact button. Your contact list can be exported into another format for use in another program or as a backup. Contacts can also be imported into your Contact List through the option on the Home tab.

161

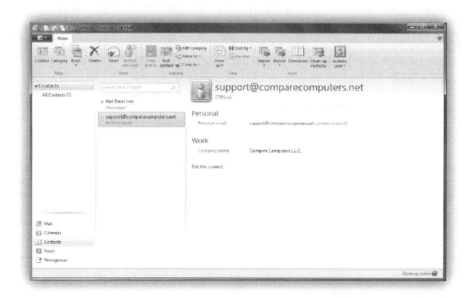

Figure 9.20: Contacts

Clicking the Feeds link in the lower-left corner of the screen will load the Feeds window in Windows Live Mail. This feature displays RSS news feeds from websites that you have subscribed to. Many websites and news providers have RSS feeds on their website that you can subscribe to. RSS feeds are generally basic headlines and text that can provide information quickly and easily to an RSS reader like Windows Live Mail.

News feeds can be added via the Feed button on the Home tab. You can delete, forward, and manage feeds that you receive through the buttons on the Home tab. Clicking on a feed article will display the contents in the right-hand Preview Pane.

The Newsgroups link in the lower-left corner of the window will open the Newsgroup feature of Windows Live Mail. Newsgroups are similar to discussion forums on websites. You can read and reply to posted content on the newsgroup server. Since newsgroups are not commonly used by most users, we won't go into detail on this portion of Windows Live Mail.

Now that we have explored the Windows Live Mail application we will move onto another program in the suite – Windows Photo Gallery. The Windows Photo Gallery application has many features to make picture editing easy. This program can be used to view, import, and edit photos on the PC.

Windows Photo Gallery

Windows Photo Gallery is a tool for easily sorting, editing, and sharing photos with others. When you first launch the program, photo and video folder locations are listed in the left pane, and photos and videos are grouped in the right pane.

Figure 9.21: Windows Photo Gallery

The Home tab can be used to import images from a device. You can manipulate images with the Manage section options, and organize photos through tagging. Pictures and video can be shared through the listed social-media links in the Share section. You can use the Photo e-mail button to add selected photos to an e-mail in your default mail program.

Figure 9.22: Home Tab

The Edit tab can be used to make adjustments to pictures and apply filters to the image.

Figure 9.23: Edit Tab

The Find tab can locate pictures by date, tagged individuals, and by rating.

Figure 9.24: Find Tab

The Create tab is used to create images based on selected options. You can create a panorama from selected images or automatically create a collage. Pictures and video can be shared through the social-media sites listed, and also by e-mail and blog.

163

Figure 9.25: Create Tab

You can arrange photos through the View tab and also view photo details.

Figure 9.26: View Tab

To import pictures from your camera or other device, you can use the Import button on the Home tab. We will look at using the Import feature to import a picture from our all-in-one printer's scanner.

Figure 9.27: Import Button

After clicking the Import button, we will see a list of supported devices. I will select the MP280 all-in-one and click the Import button.

Figure 9.28: Import Photos and Videos Window

From the New Scan window you can preview the scan and adjust the settings for the scanned image. When you are ready to scan in the image to a file, click the Scan button. This process will take a short time, during which you will see a progress bar on the screen.

Figure 9.29: New Scan Window

After the file is saved to the PC you will be able to edit the image by double-clicking the photo in Windows Photo Gallery. At the top of the screen you will see options for editing the photo and applying filters. To crop the image click the Crop button. Use your mouse to select the desired area of the picture to crop.

Figure 9.30: Edit Image – Crop Photo

To remove red eye from a photo you can click the Red Eye button. Drag a box around the eye that needs to be modified.

Figure 9.31: Remove Red Eye

To e-mail a photo in Windows Photo Gallery, click the Photo E-mail drop-down button. You can either send a photo e-mail or send the photos as an attachment in an e-mail.

Figure 9.32: Photo E-Mail Options

Sending the photos as a photo e-mail will upload the pictures to OneDrive for a limited time. This will reduce the size of the e-mail being sent since the pictures are not being added on to the e-mail itself. This feature requires a free Microsoft Account to use.

The second option, Send Photos as Attachments, will attach the selected photos to an e-mail using your default mail program. Depending on the size and number of photos attached, this may greatly increase the size of the e-mail being sent. This is the traditional way that many pictures are sent via e-mail.

While using specific features of the Windows Photo Gallery or Windows Live Mail programs, you may be prompted to sign in with your e-mail address or Microsoft Account. If you don't have a Microsoft Account, click the Sign Up link in the window to create a free account to utilize those features of the program.

Now that we have covered working with Windows 8.1 and using apps and programs in the new OS, in Chapter 10 we will turn our focus towards exploring one of the most commonly used programs today, Microsoft Office. In this chapter we will look at the newest version of the office suite—Microsoft Office 2013.

Chapter Review Questions:
1. Name two ways to attach a picture to a new e-mail in Windows Live Mail. Explain the advantages of each method.
2. Describe two ways you can save multiple attachments in an e-mail you receive.
3. Describe the process of scanning a photograph into Windows Photo Gallery.

Chapter 10 – Microsoft Office 2013

Microsoft Office 2013 is the newest release of the Microsoft Office Suite. It has been optimized for Windows 8.1 by including native cloud storage support and ease of use with a touch screen. Office 2013 is a separate program from Windows, just as it has been with all previous versions of Windows. The exception is the new Windows RT operating system, which does include Office 2013 along with the OS. Office 2013 is only compatible with Windows 7 and Windows 8.1. It does not support Windows Vista or XP. The Home and Student versions of Office 2013 include Word, Excel, PowerPoint, and OneNote. Other versions of the Office 2013 Suite include the programs in the Home and Student version, as well as some of the other Office programs like Outlook, Access, Publisher, and Lync.

If Microsoft Office 2013 is not already installed on your PC, you will need to install it with a retail disc or by downloading the installer from the office.com website. When beginning the installation you must agree to the End User License Agreement in order to use and install the software. Click the checkbox and Continue button to agree to the terms.

Click the Install Now button in the following window to begin the installation, or you can click the Customize button to change default installation settings.

It will take a few minutes for the software to install. The progress bar will advance during the installation. When the installation is complete you will see the window in Figure 10.3. Click the Close button to finish the installation. Programs installed during the setup process will now be located on your Start Screen.

Chapter Review Questions:
1. Name the ways that Microsoft Office 2013 can be installed on your PC.
2. List the operating systems that are compatible with Microsoft Office 2013.

Chapter 11 – Word 2013

Microsoft Word is one of the most commonly used programs in the Office Suite. It is used for word processing, mailings, and creating basic printouts. Click on the Word Start Screen tile to launch the program.

First Use Setup and Activation

On first launch, you may encounter the notification message in Figure 11.1 regarding the default program for editing documents. I recommend you click the Yes button to set all typical file types for document editing to be opened by Word 2013.

Figure 11.1: Change Default Program for Editing Documents

During your first use of an Office Suite program you will be prompted to activate the software. If you have the Office product associated with a Microsoft Account or Organizational Account you can select those options. If not, you can enter your product key for the software in the link below those two options.

Figure 11.2: Activate Office Window

After activation is complete you will need to choose an option for keeping the Office software secure and up-to-date. I recommend you select the first option and use the recommended settings. You can also choose to install only updates, or to be prompted for an answer at a later time.

On the first time using an Office program you will see a brief tutorial on some of the features of the new version of Office. You can either view the tutorial or click the close button to exit the guide and start using the software.

Word 2013 Start Window and Layout

Now that the initial setup process is complete, we can start to use Microsoft Word. On the initial screen when you open the program you will find the options for opening a blank document, or you can select from a number of templates available for different types of documents. For now we will select the blank document option to get started.

Figure 11.3: Select a Word Template

Along the top of the screen, you will notice the tabbed Ribbon UI with tabs and icons for performing various tasks in the program. Common tasks are located in the Home tab, which is open by default. Other tabs allow you to insert pictures and content, review page layout, and change a number of formatting options. In the pictures that follow we will break down some of the features in each tab.

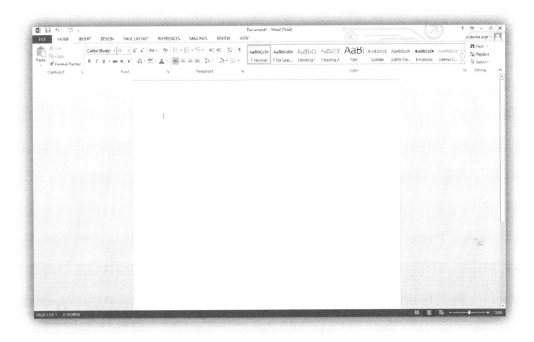

Figure 11.4: Blank Document Screen

Word 2013 Ribbon User Interface

Under the Home tab, you can cut, copy, and paste from the clipboard; adjust the font, font size, and font style options; adjust text layout and formatting; and select a style for titles, headers, and regular text. Styles allow you to change similar sections throughout your text (such as a heading) by only changing one setting. This saves you from having to manually change the format of each occurrence of a type of text. You can also find and replace specified text in a document from the Home tab.

Figure 11.5: Home Tab

In the Insert tab you can insert items into the document. You can insert types of pages and page breaks; insert tables, pictures, text, and shapes; insert apps and videos; insert headers, footers, and comments; and insert objects, equations, and symbols. Inserting apps and videos is a new feature in Word 2013. Apps and videos allow for more immersive web documents.

Figure 11.6: Insert Tab

The Design tab allows you to choose document formatting options for titles, headings, and text in your document. You can adjust colors, fonts, and spacing for document text. Watermarks, page colors, and page borders can also be changed through this tab.

Figure 11.7: Design Tab

In the Page Layout tab you can adjust the margins, page orientation, size, and number of columns. This tab can configure indentions and spacing. You can adjust object orientation on the page through the Page Layout tab.

Figure 11.8: Page Layout

Under the References tab you can set up a table of contents, add footnotes, set up citations and bibliography, and add captions. This tab also allows you to add an index reference for specific page numbers and add a table of authorities to your document. When you add content to your paper, features like the table of contents and index references will be automatically updated.

Figure 11.9: References Tab

The Mailings tab is used to create envelope and label printouts. From this tab you can import contacts from a contacts list into a mailing list.

Figure 11.10: Mailings Tab

Under the Review tab you can check spelling and grammar, check definitions, and check synonyms for a word. Language and translation options are available for modifying selected text. You can also use the comments, changes, and markup options to keep track of document notes and modifications, then accept or reject those changes. You can also use the Review tab's compare feature to view differences between two versions of a document. Editing can be limited by using the Restrict Editing option as well.

Figure 11.11: Review Tab

The View tab lets you configure the reading mode and layout of the document onscreen. You can add onscreen components, such as the ruler bar and gridlines, to the window. The view can be modified to include multiple pages on the screen at the same time, or multiple windows on the screen.

Figure 11.12: View Tab

In the upper-right corner of the screen above the Ribbon UI, you will find the Microsoft Account that is currently logged into the Microsoft Office application. From the dropdown menu for the account you can change the account picture and settings, or switch to a different Microsoft Account.

Figure 11.13: Logged In Microsoft Account

In the upper-most portion of the window next to the minimize button, you will see options for showing the Ribbon UI. You can choose to auto-hide the Ribbon, show the tabs, and show the tabs with commands. Minimizing the Ribbon UI increases the screen space available, but hides the Ribbon bar until you click on one of the tab names.

Figure 11.14: Ribbon UI Display Options

Word 2013 File Menu Interface

Clicking on the File tab on the Ribbon UI will open the File Options window. From here you can perform many file tasks, like opening, printing, saving, and modifying properties for the document.

Figure 11.15: File Options

The top entry in the File Options left pane is the Info screen. Clicking on this link will display information about the currently open file. You can view properties, such as title and author for the file, as well as view previous versions, inspect metadata, and protect the document from modifications.

Figure 11.16: Info Screen

The New link is similar to the start page for Word. You can open a new blank file or one of the many preformatted templates on the screen. You can search for terms to find a template that matches keywords in your search.

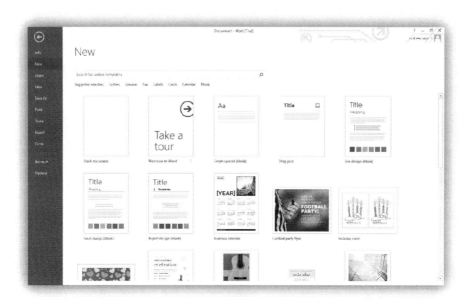

Figure 11.17: New Document Screen

The next option down from New is the Open option. From this screen you can open a recent file, a file stored in your OneDrive account, or a document stored locally on your PC.

Figure 11.18: Open File Screen

Clicking the OneDrive option lets you browse documents on your OneDrive cloud folders. You can also log into a different OneDrive account to access files not stored in the current user's OneDrive folder.

Figure 11.19: Open OneDrive Documents

The Computer link will open a new window where you can browse for documents stored locally on your PC. You can also browse for documents stored on your HomeGroup or network by using this option.

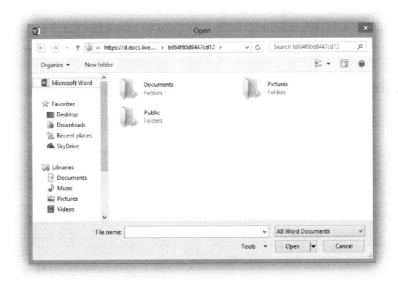

Figure 11.20: Open File Dialog Box

The final link listed under the Open option is to Add a Place. Here you can add a OneDrive folder or SharePoint folder to streamline saving files to the cloud.

Figure 11.21: Add a Place

The Save As option in the File menu lets you choose how and where to save the current document. The first option is to save the file to your OneDrive folder. The second option lets you browse for a local folder on your PC to save the file. The third option lets you add a cloud storage folder for saving files.

Figure 11.22: Save As

Under the Print option you will see a print preview of the current document on the right and various print options to the left. From here you can choose the printer, number of copies, and page options for the print.

Figure 11.23: Print Options

The Share option allows you to share a link to your document stored on OneDrive, e-mail a document to a contact, or to post online or to a blog.

Figure 11.24: Share Options

The e-mail options include sending the file as an attachment using your default mail program, sending a link to a file stored in a shared location like a public cloud folder, creating a PDF or XPS document, or faxing the document using internet fax.

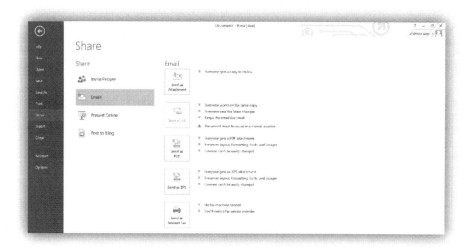

Figure 11.25: E-mail Sharing Options

The Present Online sharing option is used to present the document to others for viewing in a web browser. This option allows others to view the file in a browser without requiring them to install Microsoft Word.

Figure 11.26: Present Online Sharing Options

Post to Blog can create a new blog post using the current document with a number of different blogging services.

Figure 11.27: Post To Blog Sharing Option

The Export file option allows you to save the document in a different format, such as a PDF and XPS document, or in a format for use with an earlier version of Word or an entirely different program.

Figure 11.28: Export Options

The Account link gives an overview of the Microsoft Account settings, theme settings, and Office software product information.

Figure 11.29: Account Options

Next we will look at how to perform some common tasks in Word 2013.

Word 2013 Basic Tasks

To change the font style or size, simply highlight the text you wish to modify then choose the desired font style or size from the dropdown list. You can also make the font and size changes before you start typing.

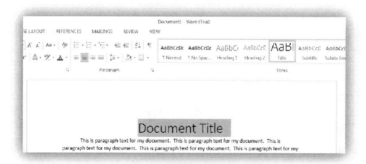

Figure 11.30: Select Text

Figure 11.31: Change Font

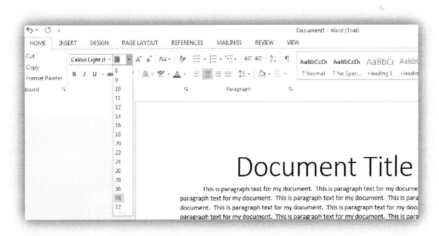

Figure 11.32: Change Font Size

To change the orientation of text on the page you can use the left align, right align, or centering options as seen in Figure 11.33.

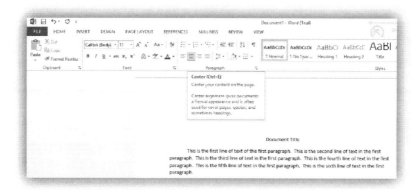

Figure 11.33: Text Centering Options

To modify the tabs, line and paragraph indentions, and line spacing, click the Paragraph dialog box button. This button is located in the lower-right corner of the Paragraph section on the Home tab.

Figure 11.34: Paragraph Dialog Box Button

This dialog box will allow you to adjust the text alignment, line spacing, and configure first-line paragraph indents and hanging indents. You can also set up tab spacing by clicking the Tabs button at the bottom of the window.

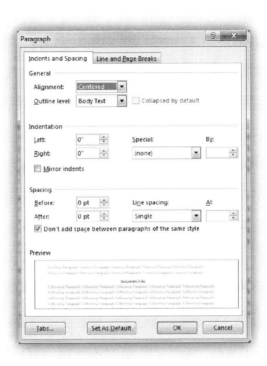

Figure 11.35: Paragraph Dialog Box

Setting styles for types of text in a document is another common task in Microsoft Office 2013 and previous versions. Instead of having to manually change the font, size, and color of every individual header, title, and paragraph in a document, you can set up styles that update each type of text with the font, color, and size you set. So if you wanted to change the color of every header in your document, you only need to change the color of the header in the style, instead of each instance of a header.

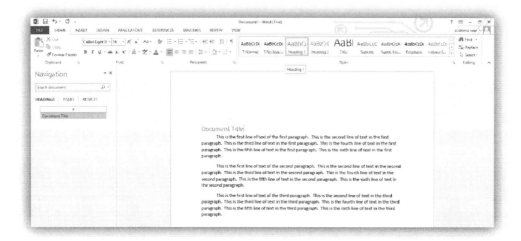

Figure 11.36: Styles Formatting

Figure 11.37: Heading 1 Style

To modify the default settings for a particular style, click the Styles dialog box button. This button is located in the lower-right corner of the Styles section of the Home tab.

Figure 11.38: Styles Dialog Box Button

Select the Modify option from the drop-down list on the style you wish to modify. This will open a new window allowing you to change numerous settings for the selected style.

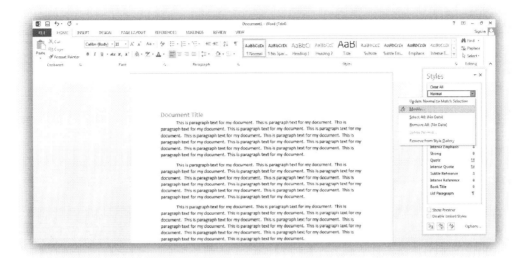

Figure 11.39: Styles Dialog Box

As an example, we may want to create a rule for the Normal style that creates a first-line paragraph indentation. In the Modify Style box, click the Format button in the lower-left corner. Select Paragraph from the list. This will open the Paragraph Indents and Spacing window that was previously discussed. However, these settings will only apply to any text in the document with the selected style.

Figure 11.40: Modify Styles Formatting

Choosing the First Line indent option will change all of the text in the document with the Normal style to have a first line indentation while leaving all other styles formatted the way they were.

Figure 11.41: Paragraph Dialog Box

In Figure 11.42 we can modify the color, font size, and layout of the Heading 2 style. There are many options that can be adjusted for each style. You will find that these options let you quickly format a document to have the layout you want.

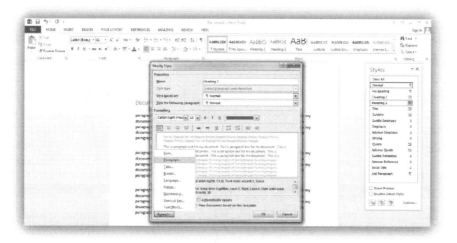

Figure 11.42: Modify Styles Formatting

Use Styles to easily make quick changes to a variety of text formats throughout your document.

Inserting tables, pictures, and clip art are all common tasks in word processing. Click on the Insert tab and select Picture to browse your available pictures to add to the document.

Figure 11.43: Insert Picture Button

After choosing the Insert Picture option you can browse to the location where your pictures are stored (normally your Pictures Library). Select the image you wish to add, then click the Insert button.

Figure 11.44: Browse for Picture

The image will be added to the document. When the image is selected with your cursor in the document, you will see the Picture Tools tab on the Ribbon. This tab can be used to resize, crop, and style the image.

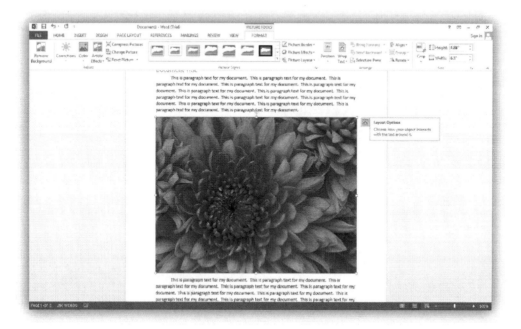

Figure 11.45: Add a Picture

One feature new to Microsoft Office 2013 is inserting Video and Apps into your word documents. Click on the Insert tab and select Online Video or Apps for Office. To insert a video you can search for a web video using Bing or enter an embed code to add the video to the document.

Figure 11.46: Add a Video

To adjust the margins in Microsoft Word 2013, click on the Page Layout tab and then select the Margins button. You can select a preset margin from the dropdown box or click on the Custom Margins link to manually enter margins.

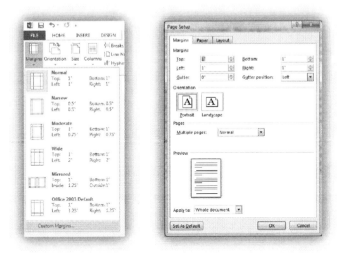

Figure 11.47: Set Page Margins

To check spelling and grammar in the document, click the Review tab, then click the Spelling & Grammar button on the left. Word will scan your document for any problems and prompt you if any corrections may need to be made. You will see a message that the check is complete once all errors have been addressed.

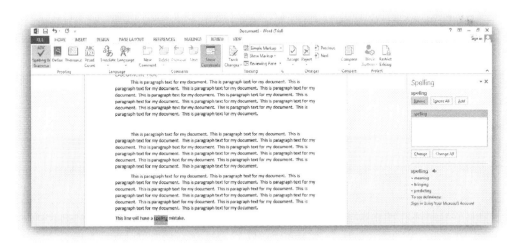

Figure 11.48: Check Spelling & Grammar

At times you may need to either locate a specific word or replace one word with another. The Find feature can be used to locate each instance of a word in the document. The Replace feature will allow you to enter a search term to locate in the document, and also the text you would like to use to replace that search term.

Figure 11.49: Find and Replace Feature

One last common task in Microsoft Word is printing envelopes and labels. To begin printing an envelope, click the Mailings tab followed by the Envelopes button. In the window that opens you can type the mailing address to be printed in the top box and the return address in the bottom box. If you need to print envelopes for a number of contacts on your PC, you can select the contacts button located above the delivery address section. You can then choose multiple contacts from your contacts list instead of manually typing each address separately.

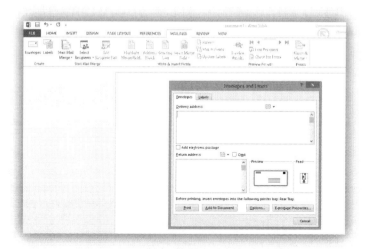

Figure 11.50: Envelopes and Mailings

Next we will take a look at the features of Excel 2013 and walk through common uses for the program.

Chapter Review Questions:

1. Explain the advantages for using Styles instead of manual adjustments in order to manage formatting in a large document.
2. Describe the steps for inserting a picture from your Pictures Library into a document.
3. Explain the steps for adding a page number header to each page in a document.

Chapter 12 – Excel 2013

Another commonly used Office Suite program is Microsoft Excel. Excel is used for creating spreadsheets, tables, and graphs. Data can be input into forms and manipulated using formulas. That data can then be used to create visual content for tables, charts, and graphs, to more easily interpret data than just numbers.

Excel 2013 Start Window and Layout

When you first open Excel you will see the option to open a recent file, create a blank spreadsheet, or use a template from the list. We will create a blank spreadsheet to work with.

Figure 12.1: Select a Template

When the blank spreadsheet opens you will find a grid for entering in columns and rows of data, the Ribbon UI along the top of the screen, and a formula bar underneath the ribbon. To add or rename spreadsheets to the workbook click the tabs in the lower left corner of the window. We will take a look at the Ribbon UI for Excel and explore some of the program's features.

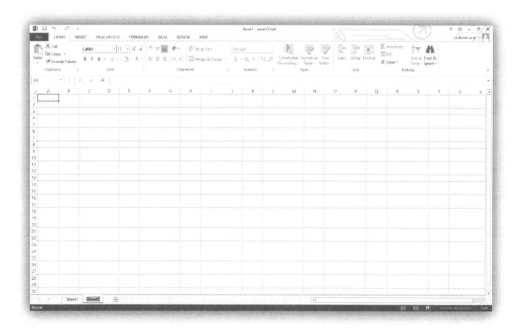

Figure 12.2: Excel Blank Spreadsheet

Excel 2013 Ribbon User Interface

The Home tab contains common tools used in Excel. You can cut, copy, and paste from the clipboard; adjust the font, font size, and font style options; adjust text layout and formatting; and format cells. The Number section lets you format the type of data in the cell as a number, percentage, or currency, as well as set the number of decimal places shown. A series of entries can be totaled with the AutoSum feature. The Fill option can fill a cell entry down a specified number of columns. You can also find and replace specified text in a document from the Home tab.

Figure 12.3: Home Tab

In the Insert tab you can insert items into the document. You can insert charts and pivot tables; insert pictures, text, and shapes; insert apps and tables; insert headers and footers; and insert objects, equations, and symbols.

Figure 12.4: Insert Tab

In the Page Layout tab you can adjust the margins, page orientation, size, and themes. This tab can configure the print area, width and height, and sheet options, as well as object orientation on the page.

Figure 12.5: Page Layout

The Formulas tab provides links to the many functions available in Excel, grouped by their category. Click on the function category for a dropdown list of common functions. Name manager is used to manage each of the cell names used as reference points in the spreadsheet. The formula auditing section of the Formulas tab can track cells used in calculations and show formulas for those calculations. The calculation options let you change when formulas in a spreadsheet are calculated.

Figure 12.6: Formulas Tab

The Data tab has items relating to data in the spreadsheet. The external data options on the left side of the data tab are for importing data from an external source. The connections section shows and refreshes the connections to the external data sources. The sort and filter section lets you sort or filter information in the spreadsheet. The Data Tools group lets you separate text in one cell into separate columns, remove duplicate entries, and validate data is within specified constraints. You can also use the What If Analysis to check the effect different values have on a formula. The Outline group allows for grouping cells together for consolidation.

Figure 12.7: Data Tab

Under the Review tab you can check spelling and grammar, check definitions, and check synonyms for a word. Translation options are available for modifying selected text. You can also use the comments, changes, and markup options to keep track of spreadsheet notes and modifications, then accept or reject those changes. Editing can be limited by using the Protect Sheet and Protect Workbook options.

Figure 12.8: Review Tab

The View tab lets you configure the reading mode and layout of the spreadsheet onscreen. You can add onscreen components, such as headings and gridlines, to the window. The view can be modified to include multiple pages on the screen at the same time, or multiple windows on the screen.

Figure 12.9: View Tab

Excel 2013 File Menu Interface

Clicking on the File tab on the Ribbon UI opens the File Options window. From here you can perform many file tasks, like opening, printing, saving, and modifying properties for the spreadsheet.

The top entry in the File Options left pane is the Info screen. Clicking on this link will display information about the currently open file. You can view properties, such as title and author for the file, as well as view previous versions, inspect metadata, and protect the document from modifications.

Figure 12.10: Info Screen

The New link is similar to the start page for Excel. You can open a new blank spreadsheet or one of the many preformatted templates on the screen. You can search for terms to find a template that matches keywords in your search.

Figure 12.11: New Spreadsheet Screen

Under the Print option you will see a print preview of the current spreadsheet on the right and various print options to the left. From here you can choose the printer, active sheets to print, number of copies, and page options for the print job.

Figure 12.12: Print Options

Clicking the Page Setup link will let you adjust print options, margins, and print layout. From this screen you can choose to print headings, gridlines, and comments.

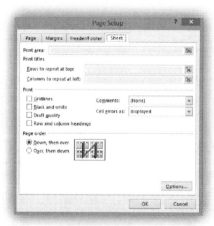

Figure 12.13: Page Setup Screen

The Export file option allows you to save the workbook in a different format. You can save as a PDF and XPS document, or in a format for use with an earlier version of Excel. You can also save the file for use with an entirely different spreadsheet program.

Figure 12.14: Export Options

Next we will look at how to perform some common, basic tasks in Excel 2013.

Excel 2013 Basic Tasks

Excel 2013 workbooks support multiple sheets of data. To navigate between the sheets, click on the Sheet tabs located in the lower-left corner of the Excel window. You can rename the sheets by double-clicking on the name and typing. You can configure formulas in Excel to utilize data from one sheet in another. For instance, if you had a sheet for each month of the year, you could pull the total balance from the previous month's sheet and use that value as the starting balance in the current month's sheet.

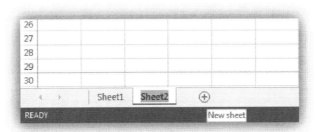

Figure 12.15: Rename Sheets

The first basic task we will look at is filling information down a column or across a row. Simply type a number in a cell followed by the Enter or Tab key. Select the cell with the text you just entered and hover your cursor in the lower-right corner of the cell. You will notice the cursor icon changes to a black "+" symbol. When you see that symbol in the cell's corner, click and drag with your mouse. Release your cursor when you reach the end of the range you wish to fill.

Figure 12.16: Fill Data

To fill items in a series you will go through the same steps, but when you have filled all of the desired cells, move your cursor to the lower-right corner of the filled range. A small box will appear with a dropdown list. In the dropdown list select the Fill Series option. The values in the list will then auto-increment from the preceding value.

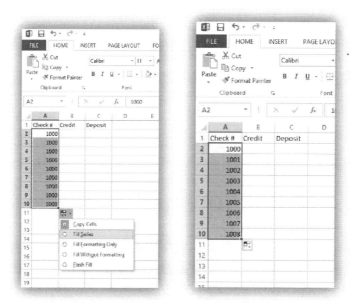

Figure 12.17: Fill Series

The next basic task will involve entering in numeric values and formatting them as currency. In the following example we will enter check amounts for the listed checks.

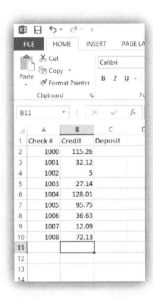

Figure 12.18: Random Values Entered

After the values have been entered, highlight the cells we want to format as currency by clicking in the center of the top cell and dragging the cursor to the last cell to be formatted.

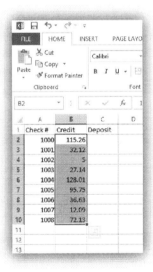

Figure 12.19: Select Cells for Formatting

Once all the cells have been selected click the dollar sign button located in the Number section of the Home tab. This will format each value as currency by adding a dollar sign and two decimal places to the value.

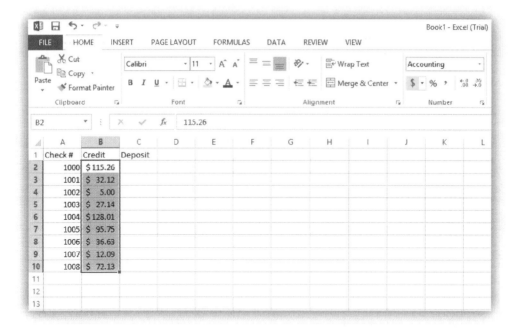

Figure 12.20: Select Cells to Total

Next, we will look at using the AutoSum formula feature to automatically calculate the total for a specified range of values. Select an empty cell for displaying the total. We will use the empty cell at the end of our check values to store the total for that column. Click the AutoSum button in the Editing section of the Home tab. The formula will appear in the cell and formula bar, and a box will appear around the cells to be added together. If you need to change the formula to modify the cells being summed, you can either manually edit the column and row values in the formula, or drag the box with the dotted lines to additional cells.

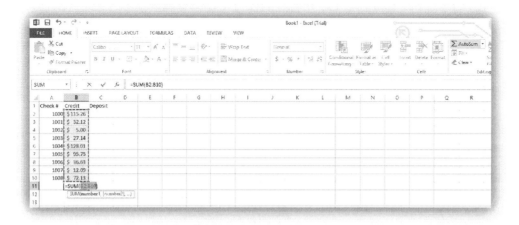

Figure 12.21: AutoSum Formula

Once the desired cells are included in the formula press Enter on your keyboard to calculate the total for the cell. The text in the cell will change to the sum value. To modify the formula click the cell and change the formula in the formula bar.

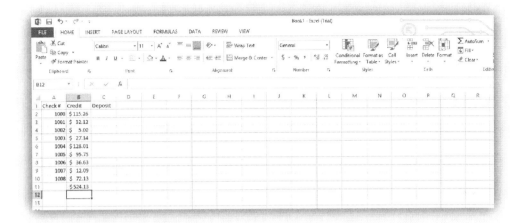

Figure 12.22: Total Value Calculated

AutoSum a series of rows by highlighting the cell following the series and clicking the AutoSum button. Verify the formula includes the desired cells and press Enter.

Next, we will look at creating charts and graphs from data entered into a spreadsheet. Highlight the data you wish to add to the chart or graph.

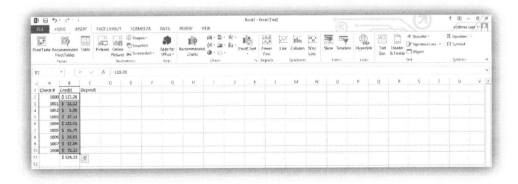

Figure 12.23: Select Data to Graph

Select the type of chart you wish to use from the Charts section on the Insert tab. We will use the data to create a pie chart.

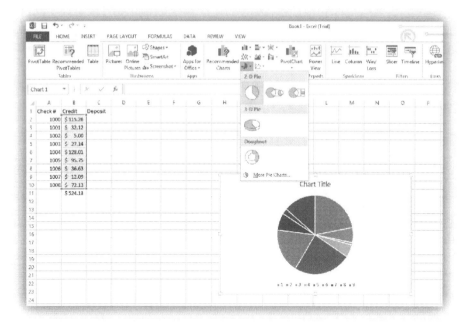

Figure 12.24: Pie Chart from Data

Selecting the column chart option will plot the data as a column chart.

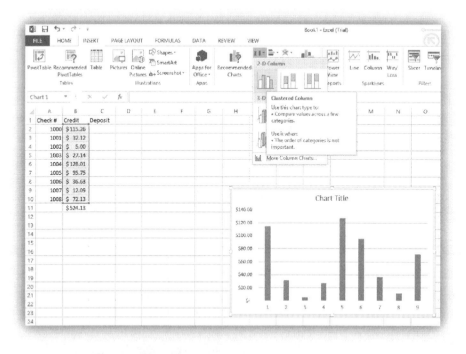

Figure 12.25: Column Chart from Data

Selecting the line chart option plots the data as a line chart. Under the Chart Tools tabs you can change the design and format options for the chart. You can modify the style and color of items in the chart to suit your needs.

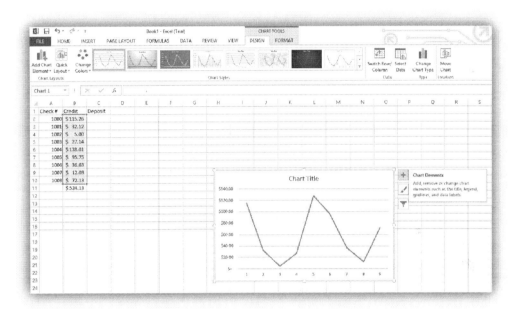

Figure 12.26: Line Chart from Data

If additional rows are needed between rows of data, right-click on the row heading that will be beneath the row we are going to add. Select Insert in the context menu that appears. This will add a new row and will shift all items in the rows beneath down one row. Be sure any formulas are correct after the shift in row numbers.

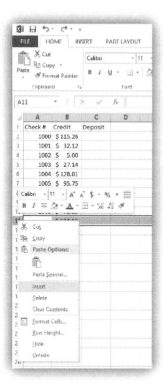

Figure 12.27: Insert Row

In Figure 12.28 you can see the AutoSum total we previously calculated will need to be modified to add in the value in the new row. Change the row number in the AutoSum formula to add the new row value into the total.

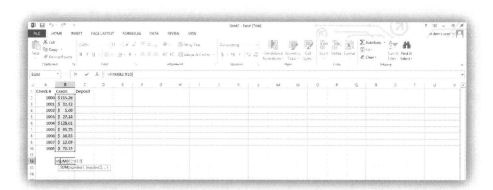

Figure 12.28: Modify Formula

 After adding rows or columns, verify your formulas reference the correct cells.

The formula has now been updated to include the new row values in the AutoSum formula.

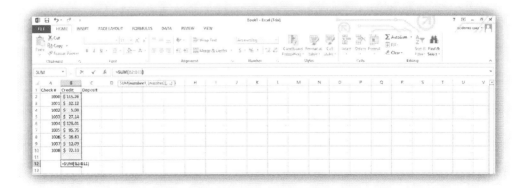

Figure 12.29: Formula is Updated

Enter in a value for a deposit that was made into the new row. Use the AutoSum feature to get a total for the Deposit column. You can then use the totals in the Credit and Deposit columns to calculate a total for both. In cell D12 we will type the formula "=SUM(C12-B12)", without quotes. This will find the sum of the values stored in cells C12 and B12. Since the value in C12 will be deposits (a positive value) and B12 will be checks written (a negative value), subtract B12 from C12 to get our total.

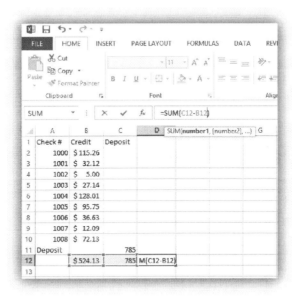

Figure 12.30: Calculate Grand Total

The next task we will look at is the insert function feature. Excel has a number of common functions for math, statistics, and other commonly used formulas. First choose an empty cell, and then click the "*fx*" button on the formula bar. This will open the Insert Function window. From here you can scroll through the lists of available functions in Excel. Select the AVERAGE function in the list and click OK.

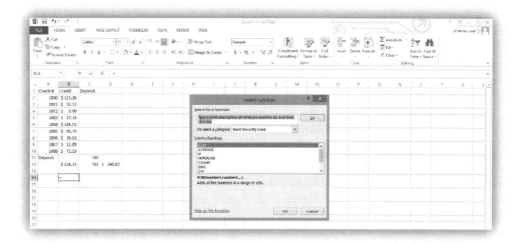

Figure 12.31: Insert Average Function

In the next window choose the cells used for the function calculation. In the Number 1 box we will enter the cell range for the values used to calculate an average. Enter "B2:B11" so that all values in cells B2 through B11 are added together and divided by the number of values totaled. Click the OK button to finish.

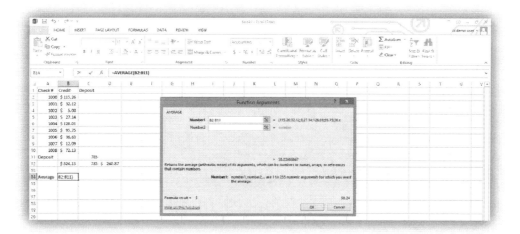

Figure 12.32: Set Function Arguments

The next commonly used feature we will explore is the Sort feature. If we have a table of data like the check register in Figure 12.33, we may want to sort out the information in descending order by check amount. Highlight the related fields that will be sorted, then click the Sort button on the Data tab.

Figure 12.33: Select Fields to Sort

In the Sort window that opens choose the options for what field and data to sort by. We will sort by the Credit columns values.

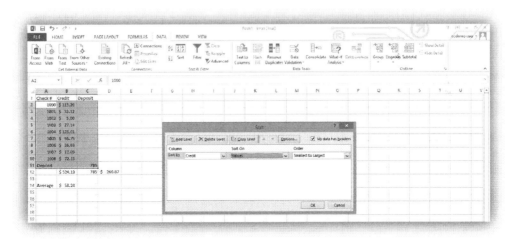

Figure 12.34: Sort Options

Once you press the OK button, Excel will sort the rows by the specified options. In Figure 12.35 you can see the rows are now sorted by the Credit column in descending order.

Figure 12.35: Sorted Data

> **Tip** Be sure to select the entire group of data to be sorted so that related data is moved together.

Now that you have learned how to perform some of the most common tasks in Excel, you should have a good foundation for working with the program. In the next section we will learn how to use PowerPoint—a program widely used for presentations at school and work.

Chapter Review Questions:
1. Describe how to fill a series of cells in a column from 1 to 100.
2. How would we add a row between row 50 and 51?
3. Describe the steps for adding up the series of cells in the column.
4. If we wanted to determine the average of our series of cells, what steps would we take to calculate the average?
5. How do we change a number in a cell to a dollar amount?

Chapter 13 – PowerPoint 2013

With PowerPoint 2013 you can produce slide shows and presentations which can be played back on a PC, DVD player, or viewed online. In the next section we will provide an overview of some of available features in PowerPoint.

PowerPoint 2013 Start Window and Layout

On the initial screen when you open the program, you will see the options for opening a blank presentation or selecting from a number of presentation templates. For now, we will select the blank presentation option to get started.

Figure 13.1: Select a PowerPoint Template

Along the top of the screen, you will notice the tabbed Ribbon UI with tabs and icons for performing various tasks in the program. Common tasks are located in the Home tab, which is open by default. Other tabs allow you to insert pictures and content, review layout, and change a number of formatting options. Above the Ribbon UI in the upper left corner, you will find icons for starting the slide show. Clicking this option lets you view the presentation with all the sounds, animations, and transitions that you have set up during the design of your presentation. In the pictures that follow we will break down some of the features in each tab.

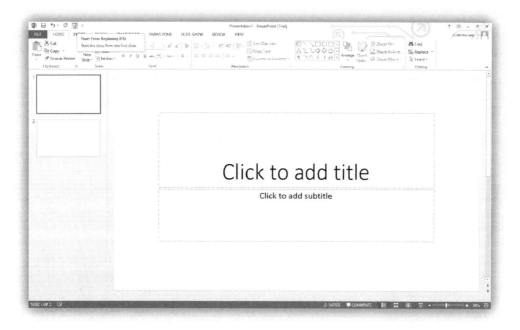

Figure 13.2: Blank Presentation Screen

PowerPoint 2013 Ribbon User Interface

Under the Home tab you can cut, copy, and paste from the clipboard; insert a new slide and adjust the layout; adjust the font, font size, and font style options; adjust text layout and formatting; and add SmartArt to the slide. You can also find and replace specified text in a document from the Home tab.

Figure 13.3: Home Tab

In the Insert tab you can insert items into the slide and presentation. You can insert new slides, tables, pictures, text, and shapes; insert apps, audio, and video; insert headers, footers, and comments; and insert objects, equations, and symbols.

Figure 13.4: Insert Tab

The Design tab allows you to choose document formatting options for titles, headings, and text in your presentation. You can adjust the background, colors, fonts, and spacing for presentation text. Watermarks and page size can also be changed through this tab.

Figure 13.5: Design Tab

In the Transitions tab you can select transition effects for navigating between slides in your presentation. You can also add sound effects to the slide show and change settings for when to advance slides.

Figure 13.6: Transitions Tab

The Animations tab contains animation effects for moving text and other content into position on each slide. Duration, delay, and order of animation effects can be set in this tab.

Figure 13.7: Animations Tab

In the slide show tab you can preview the slide show, configure slide show options, and record the slide show. You can also present online and manage monitors for use with the presentation.

Figure 13.8: Slide Show Tab

Under the Review tab you can check spelling and grammar, check definitions, and check synonyms for a word. Language and translation options are available for modifying selected text.

You can also use the comments, changes, and markup options to keep track of slide notes and modifications, then accept or reject those changes. You can also use the Review tab's compare feature to view differences between two versions of a presentation.

Figure 13.9: Review Tab

The View tab lets you configure the reading mode and layout of the presentation onscreen. You can add onscreen components, such as the ruler bar and gridlines, to the window. The view can be modified to include multiple pages on the screen at the same time or multiple windows on the screen.

Figure 13.10: View Tab

PowerPoint 2013 File Menu Interface

Clicking on the File tab on the Ribbon UI opens the File Options window. From here you can perform many file tasks, like opening, printing, saving, and modifying properties for the presentation.

The New link is similar to the start page for PowerPoint. You can open a new blank presentation or one of the many preformatted templates on the screen. You can search for terms to find a template that matches keywords in your search.

Figure 13.11: New Presentation Screen

Under the Print option you will find a print preview of the current presentation on the right, and various print options to the left. From here you can choose the printer, number of copies, and page options for the print job. You can choose how you want the presentation to print-only the current slide; all slides; or as an outline, handout, or individual pages.

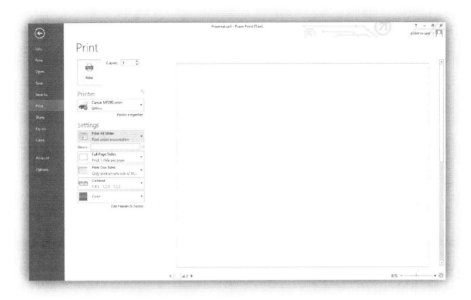

Figure 13.12: Print Options

The Share option allows you to share a link to your presentation stored on OneDrive, e-mail a presentation to a contact, or to post online or to a blog.

Figure 13.13: Share Option

The Export file option allows you to save the presentation in a different format, such as a PDF and XPS document. You can also save the file in a format for use with an earlier version of

PowerPoint or an entirely different program.

Other export options include creating a video from the presentation. You can configure the options for timing, narration, and the quality of the video rendered. The video can then be uploaded online, burned to a disc, or e-mailed.

Figure 13.14: Export Options

You can also use the Package Presentation for CD option to make a disc containing the images, sounds, videos, and fonts, along with the presentation. This way all media for the slide show is available when viewed on a different computer than where the presentation was produced. Handouts for the presentation can also be made in the Export section of the File Menu.

Figure 13.15: Package Presentation for CD

Next we will look at how to perform some common tasks in PowerPoint 2013.

PowerPoint 2013 Basic Tasks

Entering titles, text, and modifying font style and size are all common tasks for working in PowerPoint. To enter text in our blank slide template, click in the textbox that contains the text Click to Add Title. Once the cursor is in the textbox you can begin typing. Do the same for the subtitle textbox. To adjust the font or the size, select the text you wish to modify and select the font and font size you wish to use from the dropdown menus.

Figure 13.16: Enter Text, Modify Font

To insert a slide after our first title slide, click the New Slide dropdown button on the Home tab. It will expand out with several slide choices. Choose the slide that matches the content layout you will want for the slide. The slide will then be added to the presentation.

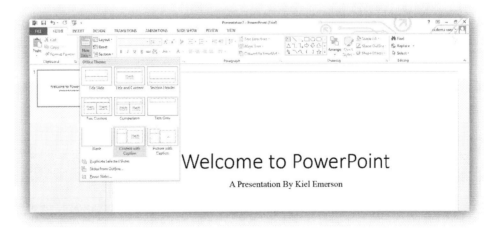

Figure 13.17: Insert Slide

Clicking the new slide in the left pane will display the slide in the right pane. From here we can add the slide title, text, and content to the slide. We can delete the textboxes and items from this slide if we choose or we can add additional content.

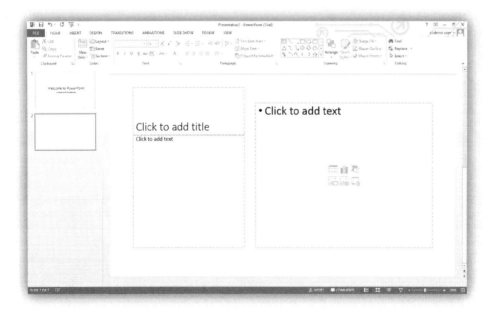

Figure 13.18: Insert Text

Now we will add an image to the slide. If we wanted to use a picture stored on the PC we can choose the Pictures button on the Insert tab. In this case we want to use an image from the Office.com Clip Art gallery. Click the Online Pictures button on the Insert tab. Then choose the Office.com clip art gallery and browse for a picture to add.

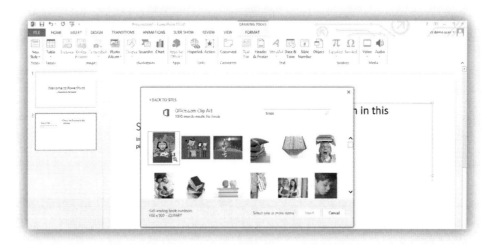

Figure 13.19: Insert an Image

After you have found the picture you wish to add, click the Insert button. The picture will then be added to the slide. You can drag the picture to position it on the slide. Use the corners of the selected image to change the size of the image.

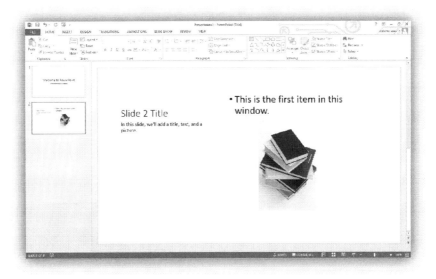

Figure 13.20: Picture Added to Slide

The next common PowerPoint task we will explore is using transitions and animations. Transitions are the graphical changes that occur between slides in a presentation. They are used to help liven up a presentation. Animations refer to the text, images, and other elements appearing on each slide. An animation may involve a line of text floating into position on the slide.

To add a transition to a slide we will select the slide we are transitioning to from the left pane. Click the Transitions tab and browse for a transition that you would like to use. When you click the transition you will see a preview of what it will look like with the selected slide.

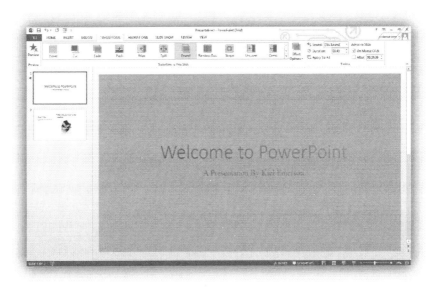

Figure 13.21: Add Slide Transitions

To add an animation to a slide element, choose the element you wish to modify. Then select an animation to use from the Animations tab. You will see a preview of what the selected option will look like on the current slide.

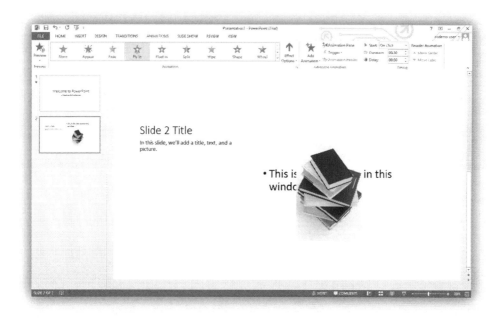

Figure 13.22: Add Animations

Now that we have learned a few basic tasks in PowerPoint, you should be more comfortable working with the program and creating presentations for home, school, and work. In the next section we will look at OneNote 2013. OneNote is the last of the four programs in the Office 2013 Home and Student version of the Suite (Word, Excel, PowerPoint, & OneNote). All other Office 2013 applications are part of either a premium business version of the suite or sold individually.

Chapter Review Questions:
1. How do we add a new slide to the presentation?
2. How do we add a picture from our Pictures Library to a slide?
3. Describe the steps for adding an animation to the picture we added to the slide, and for adding a transition between slides one and two.

Chapter 14 – OneNote 2013

OneNote is a program designed to keep track of notes, pictures, videos, reminders, and much more, all in one easy to use location. With OneNote you can use the integrated search feature to locate information quickly. You can type, embed, and move items anywhere on the screen.

OneNote 2013 Screen Layout and Basic Tasks

In OneNote, your Notebook is a major category, like school, work, or home. From there you can add pages for more refined categories, such as Science, Math, Chemistry, etc. On each page you can type notes, write with your touch screen, paste webpage content, and insert pictures and video.

To begin, select your notebook or create a new one. Then click the "+" tab to create a new page.

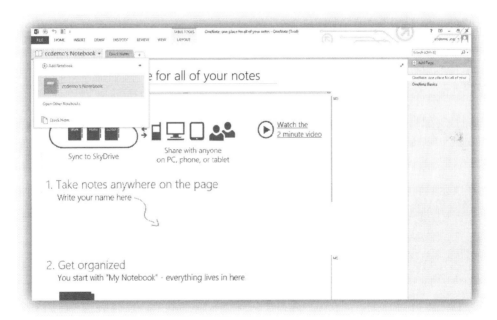

Figure 14.1: OneNote 2013 Start Page

Title the page by typing in the top section. The name listed in the right pane will reflect the new page name. You can start typing anywhere on the screen below the title or start adding content to the page.

Figure 14.2: Notebook and Pages

While browsing online, you can add a screen clipping or link to OneNote by using the Send To OneNote tool. This tool is usually running as an active program window or running in the taskbar. The Send To OneNote tool makes it easy to add sections of websites to your notebook pages.

Figure 14.3: Send To OneNote

If you click the Screen Clipping option you will see the balloon in Figure 14.4. This balloon will prompt you to select an area of the webpage to add to OneNote.

Figure 14.4: OneNote Screen Clipping Balloon

Once the area of the website has been selected, you will see the option in OneNote to select a location for the content. Choose where you want the screen clipping to go and click the Send To Selected Location button.

Figure 14.5: Select Location in OneNote

Tip Web pages, pictures, text, and other items onscreen can be captured with the OneNote Screen Clipping TaskBar program.

OneNote 2013 Ribbon User Interface

Under the Home tab you can cut, copy, and paste from the clipboard; adjust the font, font size, and font style options; adjust text layout and formatting; and select a style for titles, headers, and regular text. Styles allow you to change similar sections throughout your text (such as a heading) by only changing one setting. This saves you from having to manually change the format of each occurrence of a type of text. Tags can be added through the Home tab. Tags are used to mark items as important or as a To Do item.

Figure 14.6: Home Tab

In the Insert tab you can insert items into the notebook. You can insert tables, pictures, text, and shapes; insert audio and video; and insert dates, equations, and symbols.

Figure 14.7: Insert Tab

The Draw tab lets you choose your cursor, brush and color, and shapes for drawing on the page. You can also arrange content onscreen and convert drawing ink into text or math.

Figure 14.8: Draw Tab

The History tab allows you to view read and unread notes, track changes by specific authors, and view previous versions of the notebook.

Figure 14.9: History Tab

Under the Review tab, you can check spelling, check definitions, and check synonyms for a word. Language and translation options are available for modifying selected text. You can also view linked notes from the Review tab.

Figure 14.10: Review Tab

The View tab lets you configure the reading mode and layout of the file onscreen. You can change the onscreen format's color, page lines, and hide the titles. The Send To OneNote tool can be manually accessed from this tab as well.

Figure 14.11: View Tab

OneNote 2013 File Menu Interface

Clicking on the File tab on the Ribbon UI opens the File Options window. From here you can perform many file tasks, like opening, printing, saving, and modifying properties for the notebook.

The top entry in the File Options left pane is the Info screen. Clicking on this link will display information about the currently open file. You can share and sync the notebook from this page or view the file's properties.

Figure 14.12: Info Screen

The Share option allows you to share a link to your notebook to contacts and friends.

Figure 14.13: Share Option

The Export file option allows you to save a page, section, or notebook in a different format. You can export as a PDF and XPS document, earlier version of OneNote, or as a Microsoft Word document.

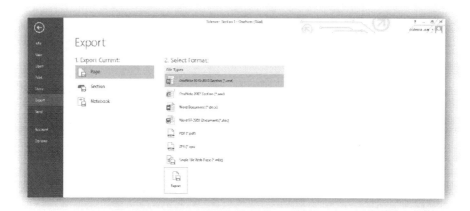

Figure 14.14: Export Options

The Send option lets you e-mail the page, attach the page as a document or PDF to an e-mail, or to send to a blogging account.

Figure 14.15: Send Options

In the Outlook 2013 section we will explore the business e-mail and scheduling application and its many features.

Chapter Review Questions:
1. Describe the differences between a Notebook, Page, and Note.
2. What tool can be used to capture on-screen pictures, text, and content?
3. What option allows you to e-mail your Notebook, attach as a PDF, or upload to a blog?

Chapter 15 – Outlook 2013

Outlook is a widely used e-mail and scheduling program that is used predominantly in business environments. Outlook allows for accessing multiple e-mail accounts, managing contacts, and setting appointments and reminders in the calendar section.

Outlook 2013 Initial Setup

When Outlook 2013 first opens, you will be presented with a wizard for configuring your e-mail account in the program. You will need to know your e-mail address, password, and possibly mail server settings for your account. Click the Next button to proceed with the wizard. If you are going to use Outlook to access your e-mail, select Yes and click the Next button.

Type your name as you would like it to appear on outgoing messages, your e-mail address, and your e-mail password in the spaces provided. If you need to manually configure your mail server settings, select that option and click Next.

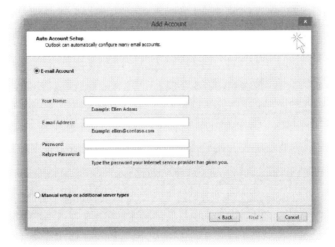

Figure 15.1: E-mail Account Information

When manually configuring mail server options you will be asked if you are using an Exchange Server, outlook.com or ActiveSync service, or if you are using POP or IMAP. Check the recommended settings with your e-mail provider for the option you should select. Click the Next button to continue.

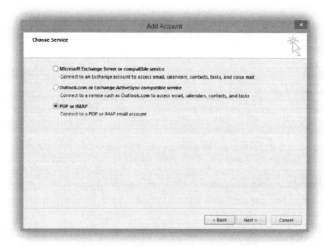

Figure 15.2: Type of Account

In the following window you will be prompted for your name, e-mail address, password, and mail server settings. Please consult your e-mail provider for the settings you will need to enter. After you have entered the information and clicked the Next button, Outlook will attempt to validate that the account settings are correct. If the settings appear to be correct you will complete the wizard and find downloaded messages in your inbox folder.

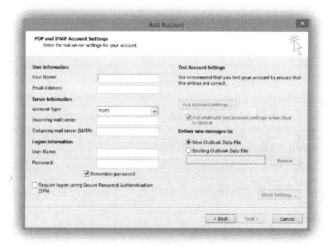

Figure 15.3: E-mail Account Manual Settings

 Be sure to verify your mail server settings with your e-mail provider.

Outlook 2013 Start Window and Layout

In the main Outlook window you will see the Ribbon UI running along the top of the screen, your e-mail folders in the left pane, messages in the center pane, and a preview of the selected message in the right pane. In the lower-left corner you can switch between categories in Outlook. Options include viewing mail, calendar, contacts, and task.

Figure 15.4: Outlook 2013 Main Window

Outlook 2013 Mail Ribbon User Interface

The Outlook Mail Home tab is the initial Ribbon UI tab that will be open in Outlook. It contains many of the common mail tasks. From this tab you can create a new e-mail message or other item; mark messages as junk or mark for deletion; reply to and forward e-mails; and move, tag, and locate e-mails.

Figure 15.5: Mail Home Tab

In the Mail Send/Receive tab you can check for new e-mail and sync folders. There are also options for downloading only message headers, working offline, and viewing or canceling the message download process.

Figure 15.6: Main Send/Receive Tab

The Mail Folder tab has options to manage and add new storage folders and options for messages stored in folders.

Figure 15.7: Mail Folders Tab

The Mail View tab has options for the onscreen layout of the window panes and e-mails in the folder pane. Messages can be arranged by sorting according to selected options. Items can also be opened in new windows for more screen space.

Figure 15.8: Mail View Tab

Outlook 2013 File Menu Interface

Clicking on the File tab on the Ribbon UI opens the File Options window. From here you can perform several tasks, like viewing account information, opening and exporting data files, saving e-mails, and printing e-mails.

The top entry in the File Options left pane is the Info screen. Clicking on this link will display information for the e-mail accounts configured in Outlook. You can configure settings for the account, add social network connections, archive messages and delete trash, and set up rules for incoming messages.

Figure 15.9: Info Screen

In the Open & Export Options you can open a calendar, an Outlook data file, another user's folder, or import and export files and settings.

Figure 15.10: Open & Export Screen

The Print Options allows you to print e-mails, choose the printer you wish to use, and select other printer options. In the right pane you can view a preview of the print as it will appear with the current settings.

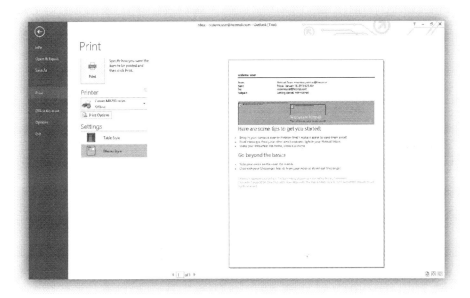

Figure 15.11: Print Options

Outlook 2013 Compose a New Message

To compose a new e-mail message, click the New E-mail button in the Home tab on the main Outlook Mail window. In the new window that opens you can create the e-mail you wish to send. Enter the e-mail address or contact name you wish to send the e-mail to in the "To" section. Add names or addresses of others that should receive a carbon copy in the "CC" box. You can enter a subject for the e-mail in the Subject box below. Type your e-mail message in the large textbox beneath the subject line. If you are not sure of the e-mail address for a contact,

231

you can either type the person's name in the "To" section, or click the "To" button or Address Book button on the home tab to select from a list of your contacts. To attach a file or picture you can use the Attach File, Attach Item, or other option from the Insert tab. To send the new e-mail click the Send button (located to the left of the "To" and "CC" sections).

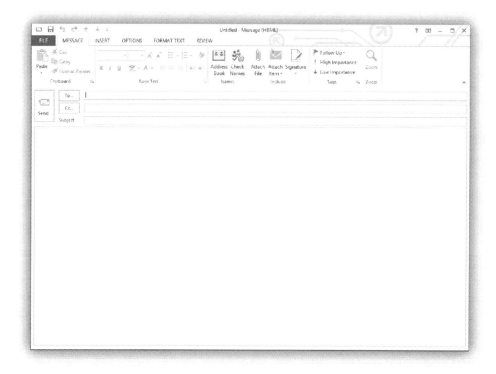

Figure 15.12: New Message Window

You can right-click on messages in the middle pane. From this context menu you can reply, forward, delete, mark as junk, and select many other message options.

Figure 15.13: Messages Context Menu

When you receive an attachment in an e-mail, you will see the file's icon at the top of the message window (Figure 15.14). Right click the attached file for options to open or save the attachment. Clicking the Open option will open the file with the default program. If no installed program can open that file type, you may be prompted to locate a program that can open the file. The Save As option will allow you to save the selected file with a specified name and location. The Save All Attachments option can be used to save all attached files in the current e-mail message to a location on your computer.

Figure 15.14: Saving Attachments

Running along the bottom left corner of the Outlook window are several links to other Outlook program components. From this menu you can switch between e-mail, your calendar, your contacts, and your tasks. Hovering over each item makes a small quick-view bubble appear, while clicking on each item will take you to that program component.

Figure 15.15: Calendar Quick-View Bubble

Outlook 2013 Calendar

The Outlook Calendar manages appointments, reminders, and can be used to notify other contacts of meetings and other events.

Outlook 2013 Calendar Window Layout

Along the top you will see the Calendar's Ribbon UI with calendar specific options. In the left pane you will find a condensed calendar for the current and following month, along with options for viewing different calendars. Above the large calendar in the right pane you will see the forecast for your location and a calendar search bar.

Figure 15.16: Outlook Calendar Main Window

Outlook 2013 Calendar Ribbon User Interface

The Home tab is used to create a new appointment, meeting, or other item; change the view style and view of the current calendar; open a different calendar; and share your calendar with others by e-mail or online.

Figure 15.17: Outlook Calendar Home Tab

The Mail Send/Receive tab can send and receive all folders and groups. There are also options for working offline and viewing or canceling the message download process.

Figure 15.18: Outlook Calendar Send/Receive Tab

The Folder tab lets you create, copy, move, and delete calendars. You can share, set permissions, and open other calendars.

Figure 15.19: Outlook Calendar Folder Tab

The View tab allows you to modify the calendar view and layout onscreen. You can change the window layout or open elements in a new window.

Figure 15.20: Outlook Calendar View Tab

Outlook 2013 People List

Clicking the People link at the bottom of the screen will open your Outlook contacts list. Here you can add, view, sort, and modify people in your address book. You can create groups for different mailing lists and include contacts in those groups.

Outlook 2013 People Window Layout

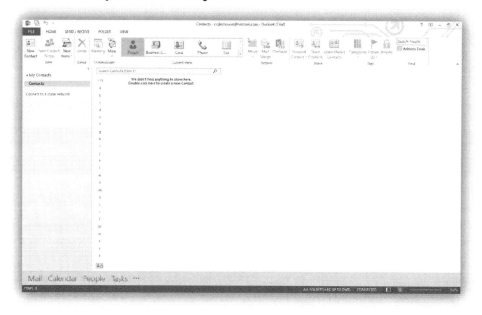

Figure 15.21: Outlook People Main Window

Outlook 2013 People Ribbon User Interface

The Home tab contains options to add a new contact, group contact, or add other items. You can share contacts with others, categorize contacts, and search your contacts.

Figure 15.22: Outlook Contacts Home Tab

The Send/Receive tab is used to send/receive all folders or groups, show or cancel progress, and work offline.

Figure 15.23: Outlook Contacts Send/Receive Tab

The Folder tab can create, copy, move, and delete folders. You can share and manage access to contacts from this tab as well.

Figure 15.24: Outlook Contacts Folder Tab

The View tab contains options for modifying the onscreen layout of elements and for opening items in a new window.

Figure 15.25: Outlook Contacts View Tab

Outlook 2013 Tasks Window Layout

Clicking on the Task link at the bottom of the window will open the Outlook Tasks window, where you can add and manage to-do lists and other tasks you need to track.

Figure 15.26: Outlook Task Main Window

Outlook 2013 Tasks Ribbon User Interface

The Home tab can create new tasks, e-mails, and other items. You can manage and respond to tasks, flag tasks for follow up, and tag or categorize tasks.

Figure 15.27: Outlook Tasks Home Tab

The Send/Receive tab can be used to send/receive all folders or groups, show or cancel progress, and work offline.

Figure 15.28: Outlook Tasks Send/Receive Tab

The Folder tab can be used to create, copy, move, and delete folders. You can share and manage access to tasks from this tab as well.

Figure 15.29: Outlook Tasks Folder Tab

The View tab can change arrangement of items and layout onscreen. You can modify the window layout and open items in a new window.

Figure 15.30: Outlook Tasks View Tab

Next we will delve into Publisher 2013 and learn how to work with the program for creating posters and other content.

Chapter Review Questions:

1. Describe the steps for attaching a PDF file in your Documents Library to a new e-mail message.
2. Explain how you would create a new calendar event and invite a contact to the event.
3. Describe how to add a new contact to your Outlook People List.

Chapter 16 – Publisher 2013

Publisher is a program in the Office 2013 suite for designing graphics-rich posters, calendars, cards, and designs.

Publisher 2013 Start Window and Layout

When launching the program, you can open a recent file from the left pane or start a new blank project. You also can choose from the many templates on the start page. For now, we will start a new blank page.

Figure 16.1: Publisher Start Page

Along the top of the screen you will notice the tabbed Ribbon UI with tabs and icons for performing various tasks in the program. Common tasks are located in the Home tab, which is open by default. Other tabs allow you to insert pictures and content, review page layout, and change a number of formatting options. In the pictures that follow, we will break down some of the features in each tab.

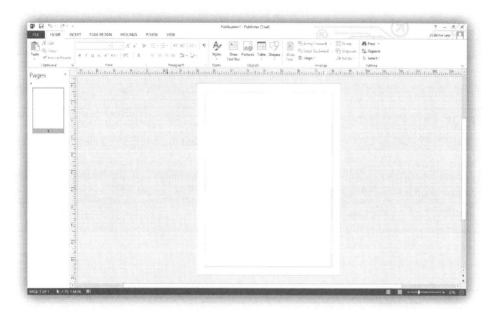

Figure 16.2: Blank Project Screen

Publisher 2013 Ribbon User Interface

Under the Home tab you can cut, copy, and paste from the clipboard; adjust the font, font size, and font style options; adjust text layout and formatting; and select a style for titles, headers, and regular text. Text boxes, tables, pictures, and shapes can all be added to the project from the Home tab. You can also find and replace specified text in a document from the Home tab.

Figure 16.3: Home Tab

In the Insert tab you can insert items into the document. You can insert pages; insert tables, pictures, text, and shapes; insert page building blocks, like calendars and advertisements; insert headers, footers, and comments; and insert objects, files, and symbols.

Figure 16.4: Insert Tab

In the Page Layout tab, you can adjust the margins, page orientation, size, and element layout. You can select color schemes for the design of the project and choose background colors and images to the page.

Figure 16.5: Page Layout

The Mailings tab is used to create personalized mailings to contacts. From this tab you can import contacts' information from a contacts list into the document.

Figure 16.6: Mailings Tab

Under the Review tab, you can check spelling, check definitions, and check synonyms for a word. Language and translation options are available for modifying selected text.

Figure 16.7: Review Tab

The View tab lets you configure the reading mode and layout of the document onscreen. You can add onscreen components, such as the ruler bar and gridlines, to the window. The view can be modified to include multiple pages on the screen at the same time. This tab can also manage multiple windows on the screen.

Figure 16.8: View Tab

Publisher 2013 File Menu Interface

Clicking on the File tab on the Ribbon UI opens the File Options window. From here you can perform many file tasks, like opening, printing, saving, and modifying properties for the project.

The top entry in the File Options left pane is the Info screen. Clicking on this link will display information about the currently open file. You can view properties, such as title and author for the file, as well as edit business information. You can also run the Design Checker to check for problems and manage embedded fonts in the design.

Figure 16.9: Info Screen

The New link is similar to the start page for Publisher. You can open a new blank file or one of the many preformatted templates on the screen. You can search for terms to find a template that matches search keywords.

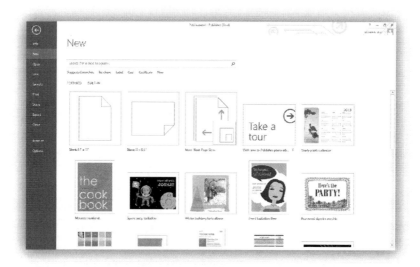

Figure 16.10: New Document Screen

Under the Print option, you will see a print preview of the current document on the right and various print options to the left. From here you can choose the printer, number of copies, and page and color options for the print job.

Figure 16.11: Print Options

The Share option allows you to e-mail the design as a publisher file attachment, PDF attachment, or XPS attachment. You can also e-mail the page as html in the e-mail body. This allows the e-mail message to have the same appearance as your publisher document without requiring an attached file to be opened.

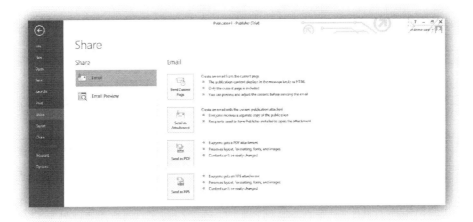

Figure 16.12: Share Option

The Export file option allows you to save the document in a different format, such as a PDF and XPS document, or in a format for use with an earlier version of Publisher. You can also export as an image file, as a web page, or use the Pack and Go option to use or print the file on a different device.

Figure 16.13: Export Options

Next we will look at how to perform some common tasks in Publisher 2013.

Publisher 2013 Basic Tasks

In Publisher, several common tasks can be used to create a variety of different projects. We will briefly look at adding text, images, and shapes to a project, as well as modifying the page design and adding page components.

To insert an online picture into the project, click on the Insert tab and then the Online Pictures option. Choose the Office.com Clip Art option. Search for a picture you would like to add to the project. When you have found the image you want, click the Insert button. You can move and resize the image by dragging the borders of the picture.

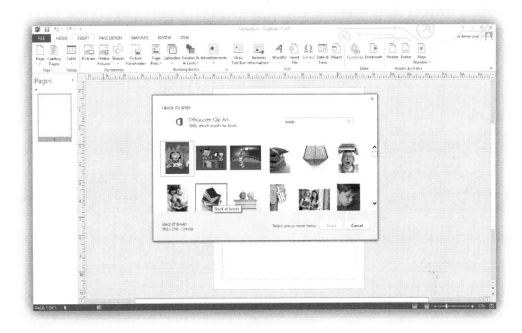

Figure 16.14: Insert an Image

To add text to the project, choose the Draw Text Box option from the Home tab. You will now see a Text Box Format tab on the Ribbon UI, which will allow you to modify the font, font size, and many other options for the text you type in the box.

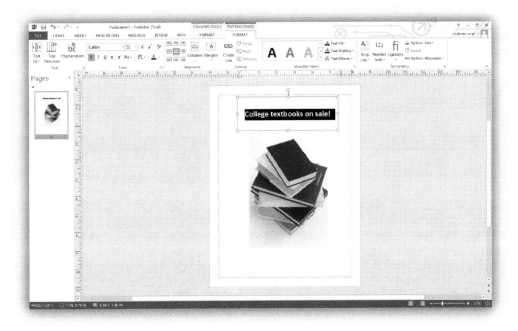

Figure 16.15: Insert a Text Box

To add a shape to the project, choose the shape you want to add from the Shapes dropdown box under the Insert tab. Once the shape is added you can move the item to a new location. Drag the borders of the shape to resize the object.

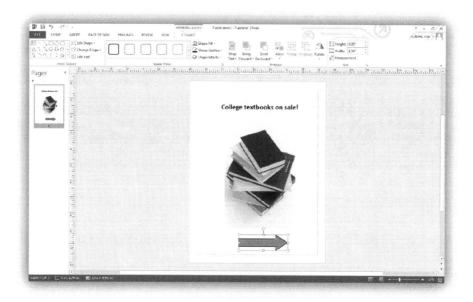

Figure 16.16: Insert a Shape

Click on the Page Design tab to modify the design and layout of the page. From here you can choose a color scheme or change the background color for the project. In this example we have changed the background to a gradient.

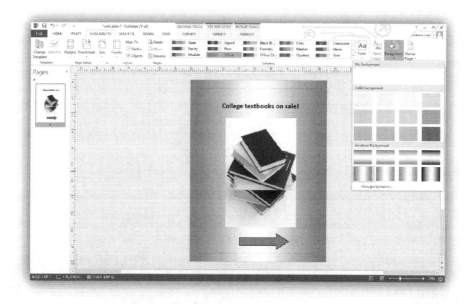

Figure 16.17: Modify Page Design

Adding Page Parts to a project lets you add some preconfigured items to the page. You can add headings, sidebars, and quote boxes, all with preset themes, to hold the text you enter. You could add a quote box to call attention to a customer's recommendation for your services on a poster for your business.

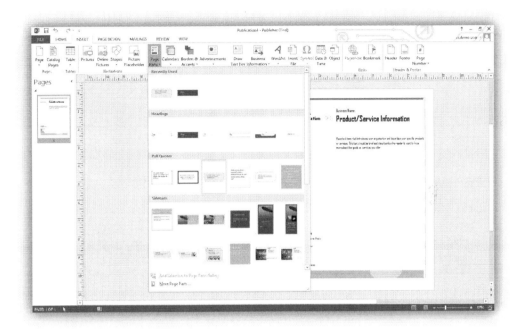

Figure 16.18: Insert Page Parts

These were just a few of the tasks you can perform in Publisher 2013. Now that you have performed several common tasks in Publisher, you should feel more comfortable working with the program to create your own unique designs.

The final Microsoft Office 2013 application that we will briefly look at is a database program called Access 2013.

Chapter Review Questions:

1. How would we add a picture from your Pictures Library to a new document?
2. If we wanted to send a sign we created to a printer, what is the best method for achieving the best quality end result?
3. What is the best method for saving our Publisher document so that we can continue to work on the file on a different PC?

Chapter 17 – Access 2013

Access is a program for creating databases, tables, and queries for working with data. Designing databases and working with features in Access is an in-depth topic, and will not be covered in detail in this book. I will briefly show you some of the basics of the program and user interface so that you may become more comfortable with exploring the program more.

Access 2013 Start Window and Layout

When launching Access, you will encounter the start page with options for opening recent files in the left pane. You can also create a new web app, new database, or use a template from the Access start page. To start a new desktop database, click the Blank Desktop Database option.

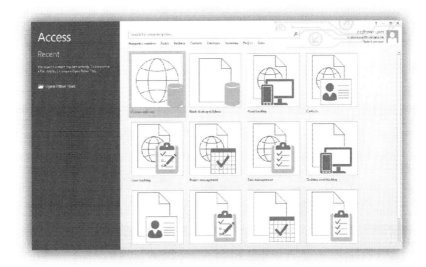

Figure 17.1: Access Start Page

You will be prompted to name the database and choose the path for the database file. Choose a name and click the Create button.

Figure 17.2: Name The Database

Along the top of the screen you will notice the tabbed Ribbon UI with tabs and icons for performing various tasks in the program. Common tasks are located in the Home tab. Other tabs allow you to import data into a table, modify tables and fields, and configure table relationships. In the pictures that follow, we will break down some of the features in each tab.

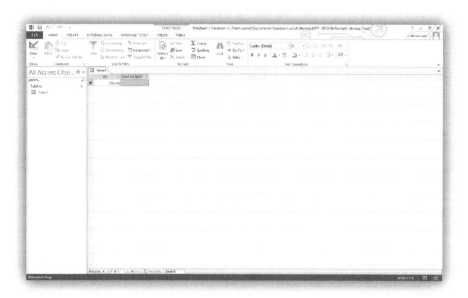

Figure 17.3: Access Main Window

Access 2013 Ribbon User Interface

Under the Home tab you can cut, copy, and paste from the clipboard; adjust the font, font size, and font style options; choose filter options; and switch between view types. You can also find and replace specified text in a document from the Home tab.

Figure 17.4: Home Tab

In the Create tab you can make tables, queries, forms, and reports. Tables store rows of data fields, forms can be used to streamline entry of data into those tables, queries output records that match criteria, and reports can be generated from queries and tables of data for analysis.

Figure 17.5: Create Tab

In the External Data tab, you can import data from another source into Access. Data can be from an Excel spreadsheet, another Access database, from another database type, or from other types of data files. You can also export data from an Access database into a different file type from this tab. Data can be exported into a spreadsheet, text file, XML file, PDF, XPS, e-mail, or other options.

Figure 17.6: External Data Tab

The Database Tools tab contains features for your database. You can use the Compact and Repair tool to fix issues with the database, run Visual Basic code or Macros, edit data table relationships and dependencies, or to move data to other applications.

Figure 17.7: Database Tools Tab

The Table Tools: The Fields tab edits the properties of data fields in the table. You can set number and formatting options from this tab. You can also choose if a field is a unique primary key or if it is a required field.

Figure 17.8: Table Tools – Fields Tab

The Table Tools: The Table tab lets you configure properties for the table, manage before and after events, and manage relationships and dependencies.

Figure 17.9: Table Tools – Table Tab

Clicking on the File tab will open the File Options screen. From this screen you can save, open, print, and publish your Access database.

Access 2013 File Menu Interface

The Info option allows you to use the Compact & Repair feature to resolve issues with the database file. You can also encrypt and password protect the database by using the Encrypt With Password feature.

Figure 17.10: Info Screen

The Open option will list any recently opened or pinned database files. To pin an item to the list, click the pin icon on the right of the database file in the list. You can also open files located on your OneDrive folder or in a folder stored on your computer.

Figure 17.11: Recent Screen

The Print option can print the current object to the printer, allow you to configure print options, and view a preview of the print.

Figure 17.12: Print Screen

The Save As option can be used to save the database for use with a previous version of Microsoft Access, save the database as a template, or save to a SharePoint server. You can also back up the database, apply a digital signature, or compile the database into an ACCDE executable only file.

Figure 17.13: Save As Screen – Save Database As Option

The Save Object As option can save the current database object as a new object or as a PDF or XPS document.

Figure 17.14: Save As Screen – Save Object As

253

Access 2013 Basic Tasks

We will begin by creating a table called CustomerNames. This table will contain three fields named CustomerID, LastName, and FirstName. You can name the columns by clicking the column title and typing in the name. The CustomerID field will be our Primary Key. That field will automatically increment and must be unique. The LastName and FirstName will contain the last and first name of each customer.

Figure 17.15: CustomerNames Table

The next table we will create is called the CustomerPhoneNumbers table. It will consist of an ID primary key field, a CustomerID foreign key field, and a PhoneNumber field. The ID field will automatically increment for each record, while the CustomerID foreign key will reference which customer the phone number belongs to. The PhoneNumber field will contain each phone number belonging to a particular customer.

Figure 17.16: CustomerPhoneNumbers Table

Now that the two tables have been created and data has been entered, we can create a relationship between the two tables. Click the Relationships button on the Database Tools tab.

Figure 17.17: Relationships Button

Select and add each table to the Relationships window. Click the Close button once the tables have been added.

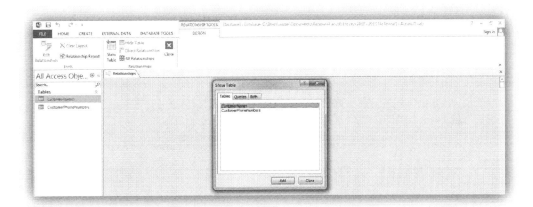

Figure 17.18: Add Tables to Create Relationships

Drag the CustomerID field from the CustomerNames table to the CustomerID field of the CustomerPhoneNumbers table to establish a relationship. Be sure the Edit Relationships window shows the two related fields in the dropdown list. Depending on your table configuration, you may want to enable referential integrity or cascade updates and deletions. For this example we will leave the settings unchecked. Click the Create button to establish the relationship.

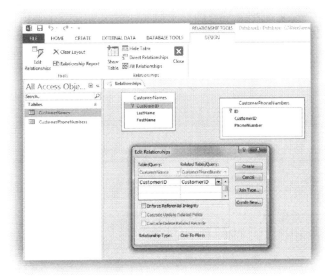

Figure 17.19: Edit Relationships Window

Now that the two table have a one-to-many relationship you will see a line linking the two related fields.

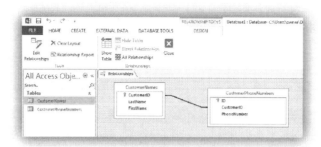

Figure 17.20: Related Tables and Fields

When you open up one of the tables, you can expand out the fields to view records in the related table that correspond to the selected record.

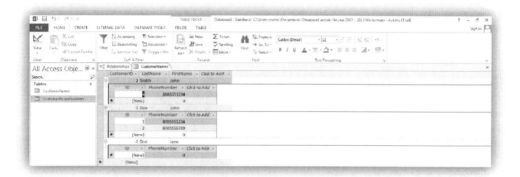

Figure 17.21: Related Data in Table View

With the overview of the Microsoft Office 2013 Suite complete, you should have a basic understanding of how each program works and feel more comfortable performing many common tasks in each application.

Chapter Review Questions:

1. What is the best method for saving our database for use with a previous version of Microsoft Access?
2. What tab can be used to set a Primary Key?
3. What tool is used to minimize the size of a database file and to resolve issues with the file?

Conclusion

In this book you have learned about the three major components to Windows 8.1—the Start Screen, Windows Desktop, and Charms Bar. You have explored desktop applications, Modern UI Apps, and the Microsoft Office 2013 Suite. You have also learned how to personalize and configure settings on the PC, manage the security of the computer, and how to stay safe online. I hope this book has helped create a solid foundation for continuing the process of learning to use Windows 8.1, and has helped to make you more comfortable working with the new operating system.

For more information and tutorial videos on Windows 8.1, Microsoft Office 2013, and other products, I encourage you to visit our website at www.comparecomputers.net.

ABOUT THE AUTHOR

Kiel Emerson received his degree in Computer Information Systems from Fort Hays State University. He is a co-owner and computer technician at Compare Computers L.L.C., a local computer repair business in Hays, KS. There he has provided support to thousands of businesses and individuals with their computing needs. He has also produced several tutorial videos to aid customers in learning Windows 8 and Microsoft Office 2013, and authored the books *Beginning Windows 7 and Microsoft Office 2010* and *Beginning Windows 8 and Microsoft Office 2013*.

KIEL EMERSON

Made in the USA
Middletown, DE
23 November 2016